There's No Place Like Home

Discovering the Destiny Within

Daryl W. Arnold

Types and Shadows from the *Wizard of Oz*

Rev/12 Publishing

Contact Pastor Arnold

Facebook   @Daryl Arnold

Twitter   @daryl_arnold

Email   darylwarnold@gmail.com

Phone   865-633-9050

Rev/12 Publishing
And they overcame him by the blood of the Lamb,
and by the word of their testimony; and they loved
not their lives unto the death. (Rev. 12:11, KJV)

Requests for information should be addressed to:
Rev 12 Publishing
211 Harriet Tubman Street
Knoxville, TN 37915

ISBN: 1547015071
ISBN-13: 9781547015078

In loving memory of my spiritual father, Dr. T.L. Lowery,
who taught me the importance of living a life of intimacy with God,
integrity with people, and Divine impartation to the next generation.

Thank you for my portion of your mantle, dad. Your legacy shall live on.

There's No Place Like Home

Contents

destiny

noun | des·ti·ny | \ˈdes-tə-nē\

1: *something that is to happen or has happened to a particular person or thing; lot or fortune.*

2: *the predetermined, usually inevitable or irresistible, course of events.*[1]

There was a season of time when I didn't have a passion for the Church or the Word of God. As a young believer, I couldn't figure out how a book of thou's, thee's, begotten's, and shall not's could help me with real issues in my life. I needed a God and a book that could help me connect really hard questions with relevant answers.

> Should I go to college or stay home and work to help my single mom?
>
> Why should I get married when I have never been exposed to an example of a healthy marriage?
>
> How can I be called to preach the Gospel when I haven't lived a very godly life myself?

In my years of ministry I've found that believers often have difficulty reconciling high level doctrine with why they were born in the first

1. *Definition from Merriam-Webster's Collegiate Dictionary.*

place. Somehow, there's been a disconnect between the heaven of the Bible preached on Sundays and the hell people are going through on a daily basis.

Perhaps that's why, in the past two decades, there has been a shift from writing on subjects that are theologically heavy and doctrinally deep – justification by faith, eternal security, eschatological prophecy – to the exploration of divine purpose and destiny. It's not that these biblical truths lack importance; they need to be discussed and understood. But we need much more than information on doctrine. We need to hear God's voice for our lives concerning destiny.

Destiny is the result of God's purpose for man's life and man's response to God's plan.

The definition of destiny found in your dictionary, the definition listed at the beginning of this introduction, is not a biblical one. It's incomplete. It eliminates human effort and responsibility. But the Bible teaches that we as Believers respond to God's direction. It is in obedience to Him that we end up in His perfect will.

Although God has a sovereign promise for our lives, there is no guarantee that promise will come to manifestation. It is contingent upon whether we are fully obedient to the plan that is connected to the promise. Destiny is more than a geographical place. It is the result of daily, fulfilled assignments by God's children.

If any of us have a desire to see our divine destiny realized, there are four experiences that we will undoubtedly find mark our journey. These four pillars of destiny are inevitable. They define the path of each person willing to take steps toward their God-designed future.

1. Discontentment with Where You are in Life

One of Satan's tactical strategies is to rob us of the promises of God and lull us into a culture of contentment. He wants us to be satisfied with living beneath the standard of God and settle in the cesspool of complacency. In his book *Good to Great,* James C. Collins issues a challenge – Don't allow a good life to keep you from achieving your greatest life.

People have become content with having a decent marriage instead of a great marriage that reflects the true covenant God originally intended. Young people are completely satisfied with making the lowest grade possible as long as it's enough to pass the course. Employees do just enough work to avoid termination from their place of employment. Even Christians have a tendency to serve God just enough to ensure they won't go to hell when they die.

But God has a plan for us, one He crafted before we took our first breath. He wants the best for us, and He wants us to become discontent with being content with the mediocre, the mundane and the miserable. You will never reach the full capacity of who you have been ordained to be until you become discontent with where you are. Anyone who sees God's destiny for them realized begins their journey with a sense of discontentment.

2. A Dream of What Could be Possible in the Future

My wife and I recently took a trip to Costa Rica. It was the most gorgeous place I had ever been, the palm trees tall and full and the ocean clear as crystal. But my favorite part was watching the multi-colored birds flying in their natural habitat and feasting on the delicacies of the sea. As I watched the beautiful, white seagulls flying over the ocean, I was reminded I've seen these birds before, not in Costa Rica, the Bahamas or even Florida, but in Knoxville, Tennessee.

They were not on a sandy beach enjoying lobster, shrimp and crab. They were at the mall in the parking lot eating left over chicken nuggets and fries that had been thrown out of someone's car. How did this happen? How did these seagulls get from some beautiful tropical location to the mall parking lot in Knoxville?

During migration, these seagulls lost their direction back to their original habitat, and instead of continuing to fly until they made their way back, they settled for making the mall their home. They stopped dreaming about feasting on lobster, shrimp and crab and settled for discarded scraps of fried food and takeout. But that's not the worst part of the narrative. The two seagulls mated and their babies grew up never even knowing who they were or where they were destined to be.

When did you stop flying? When did you give up your dreams of greatness and start settling for a chicken nuggets and fries life? When did you trade your destiny-driven goals for parking lot ambitions? It's time to start dreaming again. It's time to start dreaming of the promises God has made to you and the promises that you have made to Him. It's time to start dreaming of how the impossible can become possible and how the intangible can become tangible. Destiny will never become realized until dreams become visualized.

3. A Clear Direction of Where You are Going

There are many who are discontent with where they are and have great dreams of where they'd love to be, but they lack a clear direction or vision for how to get there. They stay in dream mode. And a dream is just a dream if you don't wake up and do the work to fulfill it. Many people die and are buried with their dreams. They never wake up, wipe the sleep out of their eyes and influence their families, communities and the people around them.

Remember, *faith without works is dead.* (James 2:26)

To experience manifested destiny in our lives, we have to have more than just dreams and desires. We have to put our hands to the plow and do something. We have to have a direction and strategy, and that comes from the Word of God. Not only has He given us the ability to dream, He's given us a roadmap that teaches us how to walk out our dreams and be lead by the Spirit.

The Bible says that a man who is a hearer of the Word and not a doer is like a man who looks in a mirror, beholds himself and walks away, forgetting what he looks like. You look in the mirror for a reason, and typically, it's to see how you look and to discern if you need to change something – remove a piece of lint from your clothing, fix a stray hair, iron a wrinkled shirt. That's what the Word of God can do too. The Bible says the Word is the mirror. The mirror alone doesn't change you, taking the lint off your clothes, fixing your hair or changing your appearance. The mirror tells you what you need to change. You have to be responsible for that. We seek direction from the scriptures and respond in obedience.

5

4. Enduring Devastation on the Way

You cannot escape trials. They are inevitable. They are necessary. And the sooner we embrace these realities, the more peace we'll experience.

> *"Many are the afflictions of the righteous:* **but** *the LORD delivereth him out of them all." (Psalm 34:19 KJV)*

> *"In the world ye shall have tribulation:* **but** *be of good cheer; I have overcome the world." (John 16:33 KJV)*

Jesus promises tribulation for the life of the believer. When we begin to walk down the path of God, when we begin to walk out our destiny, we should expect adversity. But we should also expect to overcome it.

The trials we face are a necessary part of the journey. James tells us to *"consider it a sheer gift, friends, when tests and challenges come at you...you know that under pressure, your faith-life is forced into the open and shows its true colors."* (James 1:3 MSG). The best of you is in the bottom of you, and trials reveal the power within you, through Christ Jesus, that you didn't realize was there. Suffering strengthens our faith as it reveals the glory of God's presence within us. God uses the storms of our lives to shape us into the people He created us to be and to move us toward our purpose.

There's No Place Like Home

Stories have a way of helping us more deeply understand truth. We see Jesus use them throughout scripture to reveal biblical realities. The classic story the *Wizard of Oz* brings these four pillars of destiny to life, illustrating some of the experiences we have when we seek to pursue our destiny.

It chronicles the adventures of Dorothy, a young girl who gets caught in a storm and finds herself in a strange land. She embarks on a journey to the Emerald City, home of the Wizard of Oz, who can grant her wish to return home to Kansas. Along the way, she meets a Scarecrow, Tin Man and Lion, all of whom are also looking for something they lack. Together, they travel to the Emerald City, all the while dodging attempts by the Wicked Witch of the West who wants to prevent them from pursuing their destiny.

This classic story and the adventures of each of its characters paints a picture of the journey we all take toward fulfilling our God-given destiny, the challenges we can experience on the way and just how deeply this journey changes us.

A Final Note Before We Begin Our Journey

This book was not simply written to stimulate a reader intellectually. It is meant to motivate you practically. Beginning on page 88, you will find a series of study guide questions for each of the chapters, along with a space provided for your reflection and prayer. As you read, resist the temptation to hurry to the next chapter. Instead, take a moment and reflect on what you have read and learned using the questions provided. They are designed to challenge you to take steps toward pursuing your God-given destiny. These questions are also perfect for a book club, small group or Sunday school class.

My prayer for you is that the truth of God would be revealed to you in a powerful, tangible way as you read each page of this book. I encourage you to ask the Spirit to bring a mighty, transformational revelation to your mind and heart in the chapters to come. Allow this book, and God's Word, to saturate your soul.

Chapter 1

The Diaries of Dorothy

"Somewhere over the rainbow way up high
There's a land that I heard of once in a lullaby
Somewhere over the rainbow skies are blue
And the dreams that you dare to dream really do come true"

My entire life has involved a cycle of getting lost and eventually finding my way back to where God wants me to be. Every person whether they be Christian, Muslim, Hindu, Buddhist or not religious at all have had the feeling of being lost and are looking for the path that will take them to a place of comfort, belonging and acceptance.

If you've seen the 1939 version of the film *Wizard of Oz*, you'll remember that the opening landscape is dull, dry and gray. It's here, in Kansas, that Dorothy lives on a small farm with her Auntie Em and Uncle Henry. When we meet her, she is trying to express concerns she has for her dog Toto to the people around her, but none of them are listening. We all know that feeling.

In these opening scenes, we see Dorothy dream of a life greater than her current reality, singing a song that reflects her discontent and her desire for a place vastly different than her current home, one without trouble and where the dreams she has can become reality. Something is missing from her life. Have you ever felt that way?

I believe that when God created mankind He created them like puzzles with single pieces that need to be carefully connected in order for each individual to feel complete. He ultimately withholds the final, center piece, leaving a void inside of us. Everything in the world around us calls to us, "I am that missing piece!" and many of us have tried to fill that void with all sorts of worldly devices: Drugs, alcohol, food, educational achievements, relationships, money, marriage, business success, popularity, appearance – the list goes on. But our attempts have been in vain, and at most, they have given a temporary feeling of hope. Ultimately, every one of our self-help devices has failed to satisfy our deep hunger. Although they may be good, they are insufficient. I have found that when the temporal things we try to use to satisfy us fail, and we are left unfilled each time, it's then that we start dreaming. We, like Dorothy, desire something more.

Stormproof

Dorothy believes that a place "over the rainbow" will satisfy her in a way her current circumstances can't. She believes the things she hopes for will be found in a single geographical location, and makes plans to leave Kansas behind. Like us, she believes the answer to her discontent can be found in something temporal.

A tornado touches down in Dorothy's town, and she is caught in the midst of it with her dog Toto. The storm transports them to a new place, a vibrant and colorful land with beautiful flowers and lush green fields. Dorothy quickly realizes she's not in Kansas anymore. What she doesn't realize is that although the storm has led her to a foreign land, she is actually closer to all she desired than ever before.

storm

noun, often attributive | \\ˈstȯrm \\

A disturbance of the normal condition of the atmosphere, manifesting itself by winds of unusual force or direction, often accompanied by rain, snow, hail, thunder, and lightning, or flying sand or dust.[1]

I have learned that sometimes, in order for me to move past my complacency and procrastination, I have to experience a disturbance, a strong disruption of the normal conditions in life. Something that shakes me at my very core and challenges me to move beyond my comfort zone. Something that forces me out of the opulence of my today into the possibility of my tomorrow. This doesn't always happen through wonderful sermons on Sundays or sweet worship songs on the radio.

God knows I can be both hardheaded and stubborn, so He often speaks to me through unforecasted storms. He has allowed me to experience trials and difficulties in order to refine me. Now that I'm a lot older and a little wiser, I don't try to escape every storm. I ask God for wisdom while in the midst of it and for understanding of how He wants to use it to impact my life or even the lives of others. The apostle James says,

Consider it pure joy, my brothers and sisters, whenever you face trials of many kinds, because you know that the testing of your faith produces perseverance. Let perseverance finish its work so that you may be mature and complete, not lacking anything. (James 1:2-4)

1. *Definition from Merriam-Webster's Collegiate Dictionary*

James is challenging us to not see the storms of life as tools of destruction but rather to see them as tools of destiny in the hands of God. Know that every storm that we go through is designed to make us better and not bitter, but it all depends on our perceptions. You see, we can't stop storms from coming into our lives, but we can make sure that the storms don't stop us. Storms are often unwarranted, unwanted and uncontrollable, but our responses to them are entirely in our control. We must fight the urge to see them as vices of the devil to destroy us and use them as a vehicle of God to bless us.

In August of 2005 the notorious hurricane Katrina, one of the most destructive storms of all time, hit the states of Louisiana, Mississippi and the Florida Panhandle. The strong winds and floods caused approximately $108 billion in property damage and lead to the loss of 1,900 lives. At the storm's peak, winds were calculated at up to 175 miles per hour. It was one of the most devastating natural catastrophes of modern times and left the city of New Orleans both helpless and hopeless. It was as close to the flood of Noah that the United States has ever seen.

Several witnesses stated that during the height of the storm, they noticed something strange. As everybody was running for shelter from the storm, they saw multiple eagles gathering from all over and flying towards it.

Why would these birds fly directly into the eye of one of the worst storms to ever hit the country? The answer lies in the nature of the bird. Eagles are very large birds that are constantly on the move, often traveling far distances as they seek out food and comfortable places to mate and build their nests. Although they have huge wing spans, they don't actually flap their wings very much. Instead, they use their wings to soar to their destination, allowing the force of the wind to carry them. This is why so many eagles gathered together around hurricane Katrina. They used the wind of the storm to assist them to the places they wanted to go.

That's what God expects from you, to use the storms of life to guide you into your purpose and destiny and to not panic when you hear the thunder, see the lightning or feel the rain. Instead, we can choose to stretch out our wings and rest on the wind of God.

> *He giveth power to the faint; and to them that have no might he increaseth strength. Even the youths shall faint and be weary, and the young men shall utterly fall: But they that wait upon the Lord shall renew their strength; they shall mount up with wings as eagles; they shall run, and not be weary; and they shall walk, and not faint.* (Isaiah 40:29-31 KJV)

If He Did it Before, He Will Do it Again

The storm that hits Kansas not only picks Dorothy up and whisks her away, it also uproots her entire house. Sometimes when you're hit with a storm, it doesn't just affect you but your entire house begins to fall apart. Dorothy's home is tossed around like a cardboard box until it finally comes to rest in the land of Oz. When it hits the ground and Dorothy steps out of it, she realizes that something traumatic has happened. The house has landed on a person. She soon discovers it's the Wicked Witch of the East. All you can see are the witch's legs and feet, her body covered by broken boards and planks from the old, damaged house.

The story has just started and this young girl has accidentally killed one of the greatest terrors in Oz. Maybe that's why it's never seemed to me that Dorothy is really afraid of the Wicked Witch of the West. Maybe her courage to confront the witch at the end of the story, as we'll see, is birthed out of her ability to kill the Witch of the East in the beginning of the story. Often we have trouble believing God when we are facing giant problems. Many times our circumstances are so overwhelming they seem too big to overcome. I've found that the greatest way to overcome the obstacles in front of us is to look back at the obstacles God has helped us overcome in the past. If God helped you kill one witch He'll give you the power to kill another one.

King David was known for killing the great Philistine champion, Goliath, a giant no one else had the courage to confront. In 1 Samuel 17 David tells King Saul he is willing to fight the giant and avenge both his God and his people. Saul responds by reminding David of his frail body and his lack of experience, but David rebuts by sharing a testimony of God's faithfulness to him in the past. He recalls an earlier experience:

Your servant has been keeping his father's sheep. When a lion or a bear came and carried off a sheep from the flock, I went after it, struck it and rescued the sheep from its mouth. When it turned on me, I seized it by its hair, struck it and killed it. Your servant has killed both the lion and the bear; this uncircumcised Philistine will be like one of them, because he has defied the armies of the living God. The Lord who rescued me from the paw of the lion and the paw of the bear will rescue me from the hand of this Philistine.

David trusts that if God could give him victory over the lion and the bear, He would also give him power over the uncircumcised giant.

Are you stressing out over a giant financial situation placed before you? Has not God proven Himself to be a provider in your past?

Are you struggling with an illness that has manifested in your body? Has not God demonstrated His healing power to you before?

Are you distracted by a sense of abandonment, loneliness or betrayal? Has not God always been a present help in times of trouble?

The God that we serve is the same yesterday, today and forevermore. In the words of psalmist Tye Tribbette:

> *If He did it before*
> *He will do it again*
> *The same God that's right now*
> *Is the same God back then.*[2]

Public Intoxication

When in Kansas, Dorothy felt as though she was invisible to the world and that no one listened to her. When she lands in Oz, killing the Witch of the East, that all quickly changes. She becomes a celebrity, everyone in Oz, one by one, celebrating her and exalting her for what she has done. She goes from feeling insignificant to feeling like a rock star on the same day. The problem is that it's all predicated upon what others think about her.

I've found that people often delay their destiny when they are too consumed with the opinions of others. I have personally had to fight that

2. *Lyrics from "Same God (If He Did it Before)" by Tye Tribbett, Greater Than (Live), Capitol Records*

15

battle most of my life. I know what it means to become intoxicated on the wine of other people's opinions. It feels good when you're drinking, but you feel miserable when you sober up. Many times, we end up with emotional hangovers because we are no longer receiving the celebration from others to which we have become addicted. My goal is to sing to an audience of one and seek to find my pleasure in God alone. This isn't easy.

In John 6, Jesus works one of the most noted miracles of the Bible. About five thousand people followed Jesus for miles and were becoming faint from lack of food. Jesus multiplies two fish and five loaves of bread and feeds everyone until they are all full.

> *The people realized that God was at work among them in what Jesus had just done. They said, "This is the Prophet for sure, God's Prophet right here in Galilee!" Jesus saw that in their enthusiasm, they were about to grab him and make him king, so he slipped off and went back up the mountain to be by himself.* (John 6:14-15 MSG)

Notice the response of the Savior as the people offer up applause and approval. He slips off and retreats to the mountains. He refuses to trade His assignment for celebrity. He refuses to allow where He is to distract Him from where He is going. He serves as a clear example of what it looks like to resist "public intoxication," becoming drunk from the public perceptions of others.

If you are going to live a purpose-driven life, you must reject the temptation to be a public hero yet a private failure. Refuse to give other people the key to your happiness and your heart. Like Dorothy, leave the spotlight of Oz and become the light that God has ordained you to be.

Chapter 2

Follow the Yellow Brick Road

"Which is the way back to Kansas? I can't go the way I came."

"The only one who might know is the great and powerful Wizard of Oz himself. He lives in the Emerald City, and that is a long journey from here."

"But how do I start for the Emerald City?"

"All you do is follow the yellow brick road."

I don't care who you are or where you are – God has a specific plan for your life. It doesn't matter what you've done to others or what others have done to you in the past. It may have delayed God's plan for you, but it did not deny God's plan for you.

You could be reading this book from a prison cell, a welfare line, an ICU room or a homeless shelter. It still cannot disqualify you from what God desires to do for you and, more importantly, through you. In Jeremiah 29:11-13 the Lord says to His people,

"For I know the plans I have for you," declares the Lord, "plans to prosper you and not to harm you, plans to give you hope and a future. Then you will call on

me and come and pray to me, and I will listen to you. You will seek me and find me when you seek me with all your heart."

Isn't that beautiful, to know that the God of Heaven and Earth, the creator and sustainer of all things, has a personal plan for you? We must also know that His plan does not come without responsibility. His plan only comes to pass when we stay on His path. One of the first verses I learned when I got saved was Proverbs 3:5-6,

"Trust in the Lord with all thine heart; and lean not unto thine own understanding. In all thy ways acknowledge him, and he shall direct thy paths." (KJV)

The Message translation makes it even more clear.
"Trust God from the bottom of your heart; don't try to figure out everything on your own. Listen for God's voice in everything you do, everywhere you go; he's the one who will keep you on track."

On January 2, 1983 one of the greatest hits of all times was released by who I deem to be the GOAT of R&B, the Greatest Of All Time. Billie Jean was a track that took Michael Jackson's career to another level. Not only was it filled with amazing lyric and a phenomenal story line, but it was accompanied by a dynamic music video that was second to none (outside of the Thriller video, of course).

The technical elements of the video were a highlight. Michael walks down a sidewalk, and each time he steps on one of the squares lining the street, the square lights up. I was told by someone who has a relationship with one of the producers of the video that it was one of the most difficult music videos to shoot, and Michael was the problem.

One would assume the squares lit up as a result of the pressure from Michael's feet as he stepped on them, but that wasn't the case. The squares were synchronized with the beat of the music, and Michael's choreography had been mapped out so his feet hit the squares at just the right time, giving the appearance that his feet were causing their illumination.

The problem? Michael would feel the beat of the music and do his own thing, refusing to submit to the choreography. Squares would light up to the music, but Michael would be in a completely different place, grooving in his own way and completely throwing off the video. I'm not sure how true this story is, but it sure is a great teaching moment for us when it comes to following the path God has set before us.

The yellow brick road speaks to God's divine direction and perfect will for us. Dorothy sets out on the road, beginning her journey in a colorfully fruitful place filled with an abundance of friendly people. But it does not stay that way. The path ends up leading Dorothy and the friends she meets along the way through crooked paths of dark forest, uncertain terrain and among dangerous adversaries. Walking the path God has for you, walking in your destiny, does not guarantee you will be exempt from difficulties or pain.

Jesus was always in the will of the Father. He was always walking in His destiny. On Good Friday when an entire city was waving palm trees at Him and shouting "Hosanna," He was in His destiny, but on Friday night, when He was brutally being beaten, mocked and eventually crucified, He was yet in His destiny.

After watching the movie several times, I noticed the only time Dorothy almost dies on her journey is when she tries to take a shortcut to the Emerald City by getting off the yellow brick road. When the Wicked Witch of the West realizes Dorothy and her friends are on the right path and are nearing their destiny, she develops a wicked plan to try to distract them. She creates a beautiful field of poppy flowers, extremely pleasing to the sight and with a fragrant and enticing smell. These flowers are highly poisonous. Dorothy sees and smells the beautiful poppy field, and decides to cut through instead of staying on the path marked out for her.

Interestingly enough, this is the same strategy Satan has used from the beginning to entice man into sin. He has always tempted us with something that is pleasing to our senses yet will ultimately cause us death and destruction. Look at the parallel story of Adam and Eve in the Garden of Eden in Genesis 3:1-6:

> *Now the serpent was more crafty than any of the wild animals the Lord God had made. He said to the woman, "Did God really say, 'You must not eat from any tree in the garden?'" The woman said to the serpent, "We may eat fruit from the trees in the garden, but God did say, 'You must not eat fruit from the tree that is in the middle of the garden, and you must not touch it, or you will die.'"*

> *"You will not certainly die," the serpent said to the woman. "For God knows that when you eat from it your eyes will be opened, and you will be like God, knowing good and evil." When the woman saw that the fruit of the tree was good for food and pleasing to the eye, and also desirable for gaining wisdom,*

she took some and ate it. She also gave some to her husband, who was with
her, and he ate it.

It was at that time that both Adam and Eve broke spiritual covenant with God and died. Spiritually, they died immediately and physically, they were dying slowly. Both the wicked witch and the prince of the powers of the air have the same destructive ploy, to get us off the path that God has set before us in order to detour us from our destiny. We're never to yield to the temptation to get off of God's path for our lives. Satan will always offer you shortcuts, but they always lead to destruction. Proverbs 14:12 says,

"There is a way that appears to be right, but in the end it leads to death."

In other words there are no shortcuts to get to where God desires you to be. You must follow His path and refuse to take alternate routes.

The world will tell you the only way to be promoted in society is to tear others down and build yourself up, but that's a shortcut. God says that if we humble ourselves, then He will lift us up.

The world says that if you are to financially prosper and have riches in life, you should work hard and save every penny you get, but that's a shortcut. God says to give and it will be given back to us with good measure, pressed down and running over.

The world says that if someone has mistreated you, you should hold a grudge forever, never forgiving them for what they've done, but that's a shortcut. God says that we should live a life of unconditional love and forgiveness.

It's always easier to take shortcuts, but it will always lead you into the poppy fields and away from what God would have for you. What are some of the short cuts that the enemy has used in your life to get you off course? I guess the better question is: What was the cost and the consequence that you had to pay in the poppy fields? I often ask myself how far I would be if I had never gotten distracted by shortcuts.

Saved By a New Season

Now here's the grace in the story. Dorothy goes off course and tries to take a shortcut through the poisonous poppy fields, which consequently renders her unconscious. Supernaturally, it begins to snow which breaks the curse of the wicked witch and wakes Dorothy up from her deep sleep. Likewise, when we try to take shortcuts in our lives and get off the path of righteousness, we also find ourselves experiencing the consequences of our shortcomings. But God, with His love and kindness, rescues us once again by sending a new season our way.

"And let us not be weary in well doing: for in due season we shall reap, if we faint not." (Galatians 6:9 KJV)

Chapter 3

Secrets From the Scarecrow

Dorothy travels down the yellow brick road and is startled to hear the sound of a voice nearby. She looks around as Toto barks at a scarecrow in a nearby field.

"Don't be silly, Toto. Scarecrows don't talk."

But sure enough, the Scarecrow had spoken to Dorothy. "I haven't got a brain. Only straw," he says.

After Dorothy tells him where she's going the scarecrow asks, "Do you think if I went with you, this wizard would give me some brains?"

The Scarecrow is the first significant character Dorothy encounters. He's probably my favorite character in the *Wizard of Oz*. Perhaps it's because of my love for Michael Jackson, who played his role in *The Wiz* and sang the movie's hit song, "You Can't Win." Or perhaps it's because, as a pastor, I witness and minister to many who mirror the Scarecrow's personality.

Scarecrows are placed in fields for one purpose – to protect the farmer's harvest from crows of the field that seek to devour seed before it can reach its full maturity of fruit. When I think of sowing seeds, fruit and harvest, my mind immediately travels to Mark 4. Jesus is discussing the secrets of the Kingdom with His disciples and tells the story of a farmer who sows seed that falls on several types of ground. The first seed falls by the wayside, and before it can grow roots and produce harvest, birds devour, destroy and detach it from the environment necessary for its growth. Jesus explains in verses 14 and 15,

> *The farmer sows the word. Some people are like seed along the path, where the word is sown. As soon as they hear it, Satan comes and takes away the word that was sown in them.*

One of our purposes is like that of the Scarecrow, to protect the incorruptible Word of God sown into our hearts from the enemy's attempts to steal it. Satan knows how powerful the Word can be once it is implanted deeply into our hearts. He knows that if the Word of God really takes root in our lives, it will ultimately produce an unstoppable power that is not easy to contend with, and that is scary to him. Because He was once so close to God, he knows the power of God's Word. After all, it was the very Word of God that created him in the first place (see Colossians 1:15-16). He is perfectly aware that Jesus is the Word of God made flesh.

When the Word of God is sown and established in our hearts, it will never return back to the Father void, insufficient or empty but will accomplish everything it was sent to accomplish in and through us. Knowing this, Satan's strategy is to do everything he can to stop that process from happening. This is why we experience so many storms, temptations and trials once we become serious about our faith walk and the pursuit of God's plan and purposes for our lives. Just as the birds in a field are not after the scarecrow but the seed, Satan's concerned about the Word and the potential harvest it might produce.

What is the believer's response? We guard against Satan's attempts to sabotage our journey by standing tall in the field, keeping our minds and expectations on the harvest to come.

We stand tall when we worship.

At any moment, we have two choices. We can worship, or we can worry, but we can't do both at the same time. Worshipping God is not just about the lifting of your hands. To worship is to believe in Christ by faith. When we become weary in worship and begin to worry about what the enemy is doing to us, it gives him authority over us.

When we operate in fear, it feeds the enemy. When we stand in worship, his power is stunted. Worship weakens the adversary. We see this principle in operation when Moses and the children of Israel were at war with the Amalekites. The children of Israel were both outmanned and outnumbered. They were in every way the underdogs in the fight. Yet, with all of their limitations and deficits, they eventually won the battle. How? *"As long as Moses held up his hands, the Israelites were winning, but whenever he lowered his hands, the Amalekites were winning."* (Exodus 17:11)

This is a wonderful illustration of the power of worship in our lives. As long as we lift our voices, our hands, and our hearts towards God in worship, we will always win the battle. Remember, family, the battle does not belong to us anyway. The battle belongs to the Lord. (1 Samuel 17:47)

We stand tall when we stand on the Word of God.

The Word of God not only guides us as we pursue our God-given destiny, it also serves as a weapon against the enemy. In Ephesians 6, Paul urges the church in Ephesus to be strong in the Lord.

> *Put on the full armor of God, so that you can take your stand against the devil's schemes...Stand firm then, with the belt of truth buckled around your waist, with the breastplate of righteousness in place, and with your feet fitted with the readiness that comes from the gospel of peace. In addition to all this, take up the shield of faith, with which you can extinguish all the flaming arrows of the evil one. Take the helmet of salvation and the sword of the Spirit, which is the Word of God.* (v. 10, 14-17)

Standing on the Word of God allows us to defend ourselves from the devil's attempts to destroy our dreams and ambitions. Having confidence in His Word empowers us for total victory over Satan, sin and our flesh.

We stand tall when we walk in faith.

We walk in faith when we choose to believe the promises of God despite our circumstances. Christ, being our example, experienced great affliction, even ultimately dying on the cross. Yet he continued to walk in faith, because he knew there would be a resurrection after his crucifixion.

> *"Thou wilt keep him in perfect peace, whose mind is stayed on thee: because he trusteth in thee."* (Isaiah 26:3 KJV)

When we are tempted to feel despair because of a situation we're experiencing, we must override that temptation and choose to claim the promises God has made to us. Keep your mind on Christ. Don't look at your situation. Look up to your Savior.

Protecting the Harvest

Although in Mark 4, and in many other scriptural references, Jesus connects the idea of sowing and harvest with the Word, in Luke 10 He connects that concept with the lost, those who have yet to know and receive salvation.

> *"He told them, 'The harvest is plentiful, but the workers are few. Ask the Lord of the harvest, therefore, to send out workers into his harvest field.'"* (v. 2)

Speaking to his disciples, Jesus conveyed an urgency for carrying the gospel message forward. He was trying to help the disciples understand how important it was to stay focused on the great harvest of souls He desired to be saved. Notice in the passage that Jesus does not challenge the disciples to spend all of their time praying for *souls*. No, He challenges them to pray for *laborers* who will assist in bringing forth the harvest by connecting with and inviting in those yet to know the saving power of Christ.

When I read this passage from Luke, I heard the Father say to me over and over again, "Daryl, I need more scarecrows. Pray for more scarecrows to come into the field." Most of our churches challenge us to pray for the lost, that God would send a great harvest of souls into the

Kingdom. Although that's a very important prayer request, I believe it's an insufficient one.

What happens when souls are in the field ready for harvest, but there is no one there to gather them up? In other words, what if there are people willing and wanting to follow Jesus, but no one is there to extend the invitation to them to be born again into the family of God? They will ultimately die on the vine.

Or even worse, what happens when the harvest is in the field, but there are no scarecrows in the field to shoo away the birds? The enemy will come and devour them quickly. We need not only to protect ourselves from the enemy's attempts to steal the truth God is planting in our hearts, but we also must do that for one another by interceding for each other in prayer. Jesus is the perfect example for us. Jesus gathered us up, showing us a way to salvation, and he now prays for us. Paul tells us in Romans 8 that Christ sits at the right hand of the Father, interceding for us (See v. 34). He's praying for our health, our deliverance and that strongholds would break. Jesus has modeled for us what it means to serve as a scarecrow for others through intercession.

I challenge you to be a scarecrow and pray that God would send other scarecrows to help you in the field. Pray against the enemy's attacks against new believers and those God is drawing to Himself, and be willing to mentor and disciple them. Remember, the scarecrow is not responsible for producing the harvest – that's the Farmer's job – but he can play an important role in protecting and gathering up the harvest.

God's ultimate purpose is to gather all of His children back to Himself in the new Heaven. It is crucial to remember that when God talks about His Kingdom it is from two different, yet equally important perspectives: His Kingdom on Earth and His Kingdom in Heaven. Hence, Matthew 10:6 is one of the greatest memory verses of the Christian faith: Let it be done on Earth as it is in Heaven.

I know it's not really popular to preach or teach about God's abode anymore, but regardless of its popularity, Heaven is real. It's vitally important to me as a preacher of the gospel that this book doesn't unintentionally mislead you. I don't want us to neglect or nullify our destiny in Heaven while focusing solely on our destiny on Earth. Jesus said in Mark 8:36, "*What good is it for someone to gain the whole world, yet forfeit their soul?*" Heaven is our final destination.

While flying back from Kenya a few years ago, I ended up with a six-hour layover in Amsterdam. When I arrived I went and ate at a wonderful seafood restaurant. I watched a couple of great Netflix movies I had been wanting to see. I did a little shopping in some of the airport stores, and I even cuddled up in a corner to catch up on a little sleep.

When I woke up from my nap, I noticed the departure gate was empty and everyone had already boarded the plane. I quickly ran to the counter, gave the lady my ticket and boarded the plane as the last passenger before they shut the cabin door. As I hustled to my assigned seat I realized I had made my layover so comfortable I almost had mistaken it for my final destination. I don't want us to become so distracted with trying to fulfill the destiny within that we no longer long for the destiny above. *Thy Kingdom come, thy will be done, in Earth as it is in heaven.* (Matthew 6:10)

If I Only Had A Brain

The Scarecrow's one deep desire is to have a brain, and we see him in search of his mind throughout the story. I can relate to this. I've had moments when I've felt like I've lost my mind, moments when I've thought outside of the influence of the Spirit of God.

Both God and the Devil are warring over our minds. To control a person's mind is to have control of the person (See Romans 8:5-8). On this particular issue, they both agree. The enemy is always displaying negative images of doubt, destruction, insignificance, temptation, guilt and sin in our paths in an attempt to shape our way of thinking. The mind is his playground, and his primary objective is to seize our thought life and distract us with the carnal cares of this world.

That's why the Apostle Peter warns to "gird up the loins of your mind," to protect your mind from being contaminated with things that are contradistinctive to the things of God (See 1 Peter 1:13 KJV). It's interesting that he uses the phrases "gird up the loins" and "of your mind." Those two statements don't seem to go together at first glance.

The word "gird" means to strap down or to fasten with a belt, and the word "loin" refers to a man's reproductive system. It seems odd that he connects those words to our minds on the latter end of the verse. But what Peter is trying to tell us is that we must guard and protect our minds at all costs because of their fragility. Just one negative word, temptation or deed has the proclivity to birth something in our minds that could ultimately destroy us. Listen to James as he explains how shrewd and sadistic sin can be. He says,

Don't let anyone under pressure to give in to evil say, "God is trying to trip me up." God is impervious to evil, and puts evil in no one's way. The temptation to give in to evil comes from us and only us. We have no one to blame but the leering, seducing flare-up of our own lust. Lust gets pregnant, and has a baby: sin! Sin grows up to adulthood, and becomes a real killer. (James 1:13 MSG)

A baby temptation we allow into our minds can quickly morph into a fully grown sin that can destroy us. That's why we must daily allow the scriptures to remind us that we have the mind and attitude of Christ (See Philippians 2:5). We are called and empowered to think as He thinks, love what He loves, serve how He serves and hate what He hates. Many times you can't control what comes into your mind, but you and I do have the ability to control what we allow to stay in our minds. The manifestation of your purpose is predicated upon the transformation of your mind. Let this mind be in you that was also in Christ Jesus. Paul encourages us, saying,

"Do not conform to the pattern of this world, but be transformed by the renewing of your mind. Then you will be able to test and approve what God's will is - his good, pleasing and perfect will." (Romans 12:2)

My uncle died in the late 90's after complications from Type II Diabetes. The disease affected his body in many ways. Most significantly, it damaged some of the nerves in his legs. He would often have an uncontrollable itching sensation in his left leg, a sensation so strong at times, he would scratch his leg until it was swollen, red and raw. The disease eventually progressed to the point that his legs had to be amputated from the knee down.

It was difficult to watch such a strong man struggle with something as simple as climbing a flight of stairs or into the bed on his own. But nothing was more painful than witnessing him continue to struggle with the uncontrollable itching spells he felt in a leg that was no longer there. Although his leg had been amputated for months, his mind continued to tell him that it was there, itching just as intensely as before.

In the same way that my uncle's mind continued to convince him that his dead and diseased leg was still part of his body, the enemy often attempts to convince us that the dead, diseased things God has redeemed us from are yet still alive, a strategy that hinders us from maturing and moving forward. Don't allow the devil to make you think that you are the same person now that you were before you met Jesus. You are a new creation! All old, diseased things have passed away and have died. (See 2 Corinthians 5:17) You have been made new, and that includes your mind.

What both the Scarecrow and I did not realize is that we have already been given a brain. We simply did not know it, and thus, could not sharpen or develop it. I challenge you to stop spending your life looking for something that God has already placed in your possession. Believe it, and receive it by faith. You have the mind of Christ. Walk in it!

One Willing Heart and Two Weak Knees

When Dorothy finds the Scarecrow, he is suspended high by a nail on an old wooden two-by-four stake. His arms are stretched out, his feet are nailed down and his head is drooping far down in the locks of his shoulders. Immediately, I see a figurative image of Jesus hanging on the

33

cross. The unintentional picture of the Scarecrow hanging on the wooden pole in a field and Jesus hanging on a wooden cross on a hill is an uncanny comparison. Look at the accuracy in the symbolism.

The Scarecrow is hanging alone in a field, his purpose to protect the harvest from adversaries. Jesus was hanging on the cross, abandoned by all, including His Father, to protect God's harvest of souls from Satan and his demonic allies. What a beautiful soteriological illustration of God's redemption plan for us.

There's only one problem. The Scarecrow tells Dorothy one of his greatest frustrations is that the predators he was created to scare away are not afraid of him at all. In fact, the very creatures he's meant to deter boldly pick at his straw and relax on his shoulders. Does this break the picture-perfect parallel of Jesus on the cross? Isn't the enemy afraid of that image? By no means. Satan did not fear Jesus on the cross. That was the ploy and plot of the devil all along, to kill the Son of God. It was what happened when Jesus came down from the cross that provoked fear in the heart of Satan.

Christ hanging on the cross illustrated Satan's victory over Jesus, but Jesus overcoming the cross, death, hell and the grave illustrated Jesus's eternal victory over Satan. It was His resurrection on the third day following his death that gave hell high blood pressure and the devil a heart attack. The apostle Paul alluded to this revelation in 1 Corinthians 2 saying if Satan and the rulers of this world had known the divine plan of God, they would have never crucified our Lord (See v. 8). In other words, what the enemy meant for evil God made work for our good.

Dorothy finally releases the Scarecrow from the two-by-four, and we would assume that free from his hang up, he would stand on his own two feet, hit the ground running and walk straight into his destiny. But the moment the Scarecrow's feet hit the ground, they collapse beneath him, his wobbly knees and unstable feet are too weak to hold up the weight of his body. You and I have likely experienced a similar response to freedom. Sometimes we become so stuck in our past hang ups we become too weak to walk into the blessed place God has for us.

Listen closely family. We not only need God's grace to set us free from our hang ups. We also need His grace to keep us from falling as we learn to walk by faith. I believe that many of us who are seeking God's best for us become deterred from trying to move forward, because we try to stand but often fall. That's why Jude 1:24-25 is one of my favorite scriptures in the Bible. The message translation says:

And now to him who can keep you on your feet, standing tall in his bright presence, fresh and celebrating—to our one God, our only Savior, through Jesus Christ, our Master, be glory, majesty, strength, and rule before all time, and now, and to the end of all time. Yes.

Those verses have become a daily prayer, that the Father would keep me from falling back into the sin from which He has delivered me. That He would keep me from falling into the need to be more loyal to people than to Him. That He would keep me from falling into a state of selfishness, wanting to only serve myself while neglecting the needs of others. That He would keep me from falling back into a place of ambiguity, procrastination and mediocrity. That He would keep me from falling back into the pit of pride, arrogance and self-reliance that entices me to rob God of the glory that only He deserves. That He would keep me from falling into the devil's web of lies that make subtle, silent suggestions that God has forsaken me and I'm in this fight all by myself.

I pray that He keeps me from falling! But even when I do fall, I've found that He doesn't label me a failure as long as I'm walking with Him. Because of Christ, I can stand in faith. There is no destiny without His resurrection. If life has convinced you that you are a failure because you have fallen, listen to the voice of King David in Psalm 37,

"Stalwart walks in step with God; his path blazed by God, he's happy. If he stumbles, he's not down for long; God has a grip on his hand." (v. 23-24 MSG)

I almost weep every time I read those verses because they constantly remind me that God has His hands on us even in our times of failure.

Chapter 4

Testimonies of the Tin Man

As Dorothy, Toto and the Scarecrow skip down the yellow brick road,
they hear a muffled sound that causes them to stop and listen.

A tin figure stands still just off the side of the road, his muffled voice
calling to them. It's the Scarecrow who first understands
what the tin man is trying to say, "It's oil! He needs oil!"

As a pastor, I have counseled many people struggling tremendously with depression, anxiety and even suicide. These were not people born with mental complications or who had suffered from long-term drug or alcohol abuse. These were average Christians who attended church regularly, served on deacon boards, sang in choirs and preached in pulpits, yet they habitually wrestled with daily depression and suicidal thoughts.

As I slowly challenged them to remove their masks of pseudo perfection and they became more transparent, I realized the root of their problems. It is the same problem we see the Tin Man deal with in our story, the same problem I have dealt with, and if you were to be transparent, the same problem you have encountered too. It's the feeling of being stuck in a place you don't want to be with no idea how to get out. For some of us, that looks like being stuck in a relationship. For others, it's being stuck in a financial rut. But for many of us, it is the frustration of being stuck in our own sin. It is painful to be stuck.

The Need for Oil

Dorothy and the Scarecrow come upon the Tin Man, fixed in one place and distorted after a storm. He needs the can of oil that's nearby in order to move again freely. In scripture, oil always represents the anointing and power of the Holy Spirit. In Psalm 23, David says that the Good Shepherd, who is Jesus, anoints our heads with oil. (See v. 5) In Psalm 133, he says that God will command a blessing upon our lives when the oil of the anointing covers the unified body of Christ. (See v. 1-3) The title given to the savior of the world is "Jesus the Christ," which means "Messiah" or the "anointed one." It is common knowledge in Christendom, and even in secular society, that oil in the Bible represents the anointing, the supernatural power of God that allows you to do that which you could not do in your own ability.

The prophet Isaiah tells us this anointing destroys the yoke and removes the burden (See Isaiah 10:27). When you feel you have been trapped in a yoke of any sort or under a heavy burden, the Word of God tells us you are in need of the power of the Holy Spirit in your life. God gives us his "can of oil," his anointing, when we get stuck.

What's amazing about the Tin Man's situation is that the oil he has needed was less than five feet away from him. He simply wasn't able to reach it because of his condition. The Tin Man not only needed the oil, he needed someone who would be concerned about him enough to recognize that he was stuck and use the oil to get him loose. If we look at it from a spiritual perspective, we can see a shadow of the gospel. Ephesians 2:12-13 says,

> *Remember that at that time you were separate from Christ, excluded from citizenship in Israel and foreigners to the covenants of the promise, without hope and without God in the world. But now in Christ Jesus you who once were far away have been brought near by the blood of Christ.*

There was a time when we were stuck in our trespasses, destined to spend an eternity without God and unable to release ourselves from the devil's trap. Yet God loves us so much He sent Jesus Christ, the anointed one, to place His oil, His supernatural power, on our lives that we might be set free. Like the Tin Man, we couldn't save ourselves. We needed someone who would love us and have compassion on us in our helpless and hopeless state.

Dorothy has two choices when she encounters the Tin Man. She can delay her own personal journey to help him, a complete stranger, or she can continue on her way. It's not like it's Dorothy's fault he's stuck. She has absolutely nothing to do with his condition. Not to mention, she's got problems of her own that need to be solved. Dorothy could easily cast judgment on the Tin Man, because he should have known that if he were to get wet, he would eventually rust out. After all, he is made out of tin. Why not take the necessary precautions?

But rather than casting judgment and continuing on her way, she stops. Maybe it's because she realizes through her own experience that sometimes you get stuck in storms you have no control of at all.

Sometimes storms will escape the weatherman's forecast. Sometimes storms come unannounced, uninvited and unwanted.

That's why you and I can't judge another. We never know why a person is in their current condition. Something doesn't have to be your fault for it to be your problem. This morning, a baby was born addicted to drugs without ever smoking a crack pipe or snorting a line of cocaine. There is a woman struggling to raise her children and barely making ends meet, because her husband left her for another woman. There is a man who went to the doctor for his annual checkup and discovered he is dying from lung cancer, yet he has never had a cigarette in his mouth. There is a little girl who has been molested by a family member and is constantly being tormented by memories of the attack. Someone's situation doesn't have to be their fault for it to be their problem.

Oftentimes, life can be challenging, unfair and in many instances, outright evil. But that's why God gives us the oil, the power of the Spirit that is beyond any strength we have on our own. There is no challenge life can set before us that the anointing cannot fix.

After she retrieves the can of oil, Dorothy asks the Tin Man, "Where do you want me to place the oil first?" If it were me, and I'd been stuck in the same place for so long, I probably would have said my legs or arms. But that is not his request. "My mouth. Oil my mouth first." He knew that if he could get his mouth loose, he could clearly articulate to Dorothy which other areas of his body he needed her to loosen.

Let's think for a second. Who's to say that other people who had compassionate hearts had not also passed down that very same yellow brick road before and had not stopped to help? Maybe it's not that they refused to help him. Maybe they didn't realize he was stuck. Perhaps they walked right by him, because he could not open up his mouth to get their attention. You have no idea how many people who are part of your everyday life are hurting but refuse to ask for help.

Many of us are broken, battered and bruised, yet the enemy has rusted us out, so we can't open up our mouths to get help. The last thing Satan wants is for you to somehow get some oil on your mouth. He knows that if you get your mouth loose, every other area of your life can be loosened too. He knows that once we begin asking for oil, the supernatural power of God, there is nothing he can do.

In John 5, the writer tells the story of a man who has been lame for 38 years. (See v. 1-8) Although a multitude of people were around him, no one would help him. Not unlike the Tin Man, this lame man was stuck. Jesus was walking by, noticed his infirmity, and asked him, "Do you want to be made whole?" Jesus did not lay hands on his legs or feet or preach a sermon to him. Jesus began the miracle by trying to get oil on the man's mouth, to get him to acknowledge his need for healing. He wanted this man to begin speaking faith over his own body.

Instead of responding with an emphatic "yes," the man complains about his physical state and the people around him. Although the mercy of God still healed the lame man, this was not the divine model of how Jesus wanted it done. He wanted this man to understand that the power of death and life was in his tongue. In the same way, He wants us to place oil on our mouths and speak about where we are headed in the future and not where we may be stuck in the present.

If you get your mouth loose, it will get your finances loose.
My God shall supply all of my needs according to His riches in glory.
(Philippians 4:19)

If you get your mouth loose, it will get your body loose.
By His stripes we are healed. (Isaiah 53:5)

If you get your mouth loose, it will get your family loose.
As for me and my house we shall serve the Lord. (Joshua 24:15)

If you get your mouth loose, it will get your soul loose.
If you confess with your mouth and believe with your heart that God has raised His Son from the grave you shall be saved. (Romans 10:9)

Our mouths have the power to change our circumstances.

My family and I moved into a home several years ago in a small, quiet neighborhood on the outskirts of the city. I loved that the home sat in a rural community. My wife was excited we finally had enough room for all of the children. But what my two-year-old son liked the most was the community swimming pool located at the entrance of the neighborhood. As we drove up in the subdivision my son asked me if the pool was ours.

"Yes, Timbreland. It's ours."

"Then will you take me swimming in it?"

"Yes, son. I'll take you swimming."

By the time we made it to bed that night he had already asked me the same question three times. Right before he closed his eyes to sleep he asked me once again,

"Daddy, will you take me swimming?"

"Yes, Timbreland, I promise. Now go to bed!"

I woke up early the next morning and put in a long, productive day of work. When I pulled up to my driveway, I was surprised to be met by my two-year-old son on the front porch, his shirt off, a swimming diaper on and a towel around his neck. It was mid-December. I quickly picked him up and took him out of the cold.

My oldest daughter said to me, "Daddy, we tried to tell him that you weren't taking him swimming, but he wouldn't listen to us. He just kept saying that if his daddy promised him, his daddy wouldn't let him down."

When I heard what he had said I was both flattered and convicted, flattered to know my son had so much confidence in the character of his father he knew I wouldn't break my promise to him, and convicted, because I knew I didn't have the same level of confidence in my heavenly Father to know that He would never break a promise He has made to me.

My son taught me two things that day I will never forget. First, if my Father makes a promise to me, He is willing and able to fulfill it. Second, God does not have to wait for a certain season to come around before He can bless me. This is why no matter what obstacles may be in my way, I choose to focus not on what could hinder me, but keep the promises of God in my mouth instead.

Whatever the trial may be, my brother and sister, if you keep asking for the oil, the supernatural power of God, you may get stuck but you won't stay stuck for long. The enemy will still send storms your way in an attempt to rust you out, but you must not quit. You have to do what the Tin Man does after he is loosened by Dorothy. He carries the oil can with him everywhere he goes, and when he feels like he is getting stuck, he oils himself all over again.

If I Only Had A Heart

Like the Scarecrow, the Tin Man has a sense of insecurity because he feels something is missing in his life. He shares with Dorothy and the Scarecrow his desperate desire to have a heart. Though he's adamant he lacks one, everything about his character and actions throughout the story suggests he already has a heart and that it is beating just fine. Every time the wicked witch or her flying monkeys do something to try to harm Dorothy, he cries out with compassion. When Dorothy becomes homesick, he always says something comforting to cheer her up. He shows acts of kindness and expresses love for those who are hurting.

So, where does he get the impression that he doesn't have a heart? How would he even know if he had one since the heart is on the inside of a person? Perhaps it was because he could only see the outside of himself that he believed he was a heartless person.

The Tin Man was made up of several discarded pieces of scrap tin and metal. His entire existence was basically a conglomeration of extra pieces of junk left over from more significant projects. Maybe when the Tin Man looked at all of his flaws, imperfections and inconsistencies in the mirror, he came to the conclusion that his maker would never put something as valuable as a heart in something as invaluable as a body made of old junk.

My friend, haven't we all been there? If the truth were told, many of you reading this book right now are there, stuck on the side of the yellow brick road with a Tin Man mentality, unable to believe that God would put anything of real significance or value within you. But we see in scripture and in life today that God often chooses the foolish things of this world to confound the wise (1 Corinthians 1:27).

Throughout the Bible, we see that when God is looking to build something great, he doesn't get His materials from Lowe's, Home Depot or any other brand name hardware store. He gets all of His materials from the junkyard. He doesn't always choose the smartest or most qualified person. He uses average people to do His work and build the Kingdom. Why? He wants to ensure that when He uses us, no one will receive glory except for Him.

Paul says in 2 Corinthians 4:7, *"But we have this treasure in jars of clay to show that this all-surpassing power is from God and not from us."* There's nothing beautiful or special about a simple clay pot. It's the treasure that gives the clay vessel its value. God has not made you valuable because of who you are or what you've done. Your value has come from the Spirit He has so graciously deposited within you through the shed blood of Jesus Christ.

The word "heart" is mentioned in the King James Bible over 740 times. I believe God uses the biological image of the heart to illustrate a theological principle. God has made our physical bodies so durable, they are able to recover from all sorts of accidents, injuries and disease.

I know people who are living with one kidney, some with only one lung, and some who have gone completely blind. I have seen people who are quadruple amputees and still live healthy, productive lives. However, I have never met a person who is living without a heart. When the heart is no longer working, it will cause death instantaneously. In the Bible, the heart is used as a metaphor to illustrate that a man's soul must be pure and healthy in order for him to have spiritual life.

A person's heart is the most important organ, because it's primary objective is to keep the blood flowing throughout the rest of the body. Wherever the blood does not flow will eventually die. The life of a person is in the blood. This is why God gives us not only a redeemed heart but a renewed heart. He gives us the heart of His Son so that the blood of Christ can flow through our bodies and give us eternal and abundant life. God did not just create you with a heart, but through the redemption process, He gave us *His* heart.

I had been preaching the gospel for years before this reality actually sank into my own soul. I understood it in my head but didn't fully receive it in my heart until God revealed it to me so clearly. I was watching *John Q*, a 2002 movie about a little boy who learns he has heart disease and will not be able to live without a heart transplant. His father, played by Denzel Washington, does not have insurance, and the hospital refuses to put him on the donors list. The father is so desperate to save his son, he takes everyone in the hospital hostage, demanding his son receive a heart.

As his son begins to die, the father puts a gun to his own head and tells the surgeon that after he kills himself, he wants the surgeon to take out his heart and give it to his child so that he can live. With tears in his eyes, the father puts his hand over his dying son's chest and says, "I will never leave, son. I'll always be right here with you in your heart."

When I saw this scene, I finally got it. I was the little boy who had the bad heart, a heart that was killing me. But Jesus loved me so much that he died for me on the cross and gave me His heart that I might live. Not only did He do this for me, He did it for the entire world.

He had to do it in order for any of us to have a chance at eternal life. Jeremiah 17:19 says, *"The heart of man is deceitful above all things and beyond cure. Who can understand it?"* In Mark 7:21-23, Jesus defines the condition of man's heart outside of His saving grace. He says,

For it is from within, out of a person's heart, that evil thoughts come—sexual immorality, theft, murder, adultery, greed, malice, deceit, lewdness, envy, slander, arrogance and folly. All these evils come from inside and defile a person.

Every person on this planet has to have a spiritual heart transplant if they are going to have eternal life. However, there is some good news. It's available to everyone, regardless of what you've done in the past or even what you're doing right now.

What you did wrong last year, last month, last week or even last night will not disqualify you from Jesus's heart transplant list. Maybe you can't remember a time when you asked the Father to give you a new heart. If that's true, the grace of God is so awesome, He will save you from your sins and give you a new, clean heart. If you are sincere and ready to have a completely new life, pray this prayer with me.

Father, I have made some serious mistakes in my life and have sinned against you. I now realize that your love for me is greater than the mistakes I have made. So, I ask you to forgive me. I believe that you sent your Son to the cross to pay for all of my failures and then raised Him from the grave, so that I could have eternal life. Thank you for giving me a new chance, a new start and a new heart. I'm saved! Amen.

If you just prayed that prayer you have been given the heart of Jesus, and His blood will be flowing throughout your life from this day forward. Don't let the rust marks on your tin body, the past mistakes or wounds in your life, mislead you. They are merely testimonies of who you were before you received your new heart. Not only did you receive a new heart that has the ability to be loved by God, but you also have a new heart that has the ability to love like God.

Chapter 5

Lessons from the Cowardly Lion

Dorothy and her friends skip into a dark forest. They begin to worry they might see "lions and tigers and bears, oh my!"

Just as they feared, they hear a terrifying roar, and a large lion leaps into their path.

But all was not as it seemed. When Dorothy bravely confronts him, the lion's eyes fill with tears and he shrinks back in fear.

I have found that, generally speaking, when people are loud, obnoxious and overly aggressive toward others, it's a sign they are struggling with some form of deep fear. The person with the loudest roar is usually the person who is most afraid. In our story, the Cowardly Lion roars to scare off his adversaries, because he is too afraid to confront them. Many times the intimidator is actually the intimidated. They try to appear strong externally in an attempt to mask the fear that dwells deep inside of them.

For years, I never thought there was anything wrong with being fearful or timid. I assumed it was a natural human emotion that everyone has to deal with from time to time. During a daily devotional one day, I ran across a couple of scriptures in Revelation that shook my very foundation and overturned what I believed about fear.

It is done. I am the Alpha and the Omega, the Beginning and the End. To the thirsty I will give water without cost from the spring of the water of life. Those who are victorious will inherit all this, and I will be their God and they will be my children. But the cowardly, the unbelieving, the vile, the murderers, the sexually immoral, those who practice magic arts, the idolaters and all liars—they will be consigned to the fiery lake of burning sulfur. This is the second death. " (Revelation 21:6-8)

In this passage, John the Revelator presents a long list of abominable sins that separate us from the presence of God and are at odds with God's character of holiness. He does not list every aspect of the depravity of man, but he does mention several things that he considers so repulsive to God that those who embrace them without ultimately embracing God's grace, will eventually be lost forever as a consequence.

He talks about murderers who have viciously taken someone's life. He talks about the sexually immoral who are living perverted lives; those cheating on their spouses with no remorse, those living homosexual lifestyles with no repentance, those who have raped and violated the innocent, those who have violently molested little children. He talks about the idol worshippers and magic workers; those who have placed their confidence in vu du, ouija boards, horoscopes, palm readers, witch doctors, black religions, séances, fortune telling, satanism and doctrines of devils. He talks about the vile; those who constantly have their focus and imagination on evil, wickedness, mischief and filthy activity.

In that very same list of deeds overtly offensive to the character of God, John includes the cowardly or the fearful. Not only does he include the cowards, but he places them at the top of the list of evildoers. I realize that more than likely, you haven't murdered anyone, may not be living a sexually immoral life and haven't engaged in voodoo or witchcraft. But most people reading this book, myself included, have struggled with the sin of walking in fear and timidity.

Perhaps like the Cowardly Lion, we purposely roar loud to keep others at a distance, so they will never notice how frightened and fragile we can really be. Many of us have mastered the art of roaring like a lion on the outside only to cover up the cowardly kitty cat that is trapped within.

What's the thing that causes the most tension and anxiety in your life? Is it the fear of becoming a failure? Is it the fear of not accomplishing your goals in life or meeting up to the expectations of those you admire? Is it the fear of not being a good parent or a good child? Is it the fear of moving into ministry or starting the business you have been dreaming about for years and failing miserably? Is it the fear of going back to school and getting your degree? Is it the fear of going to the doctor, because you have experienced some unusual symptoms? Is it the fear of getting out of a relationship that feels good to you but you know is not good for you? Is it the fear of stepping into a new endeavor you're certain you are neither equipped nor qualified for?

Whatever shape, form or fashion fear has taken in your life, it is still no match for the God who lives within you. Perfect love really does cast out all fear. (1 John 4:18) The more you understand how perfect God's love is for you the more fully you will believe He will never let you down. Fear comes from the uncertainty that things are going to work out on your behalf. I am a witness that even when the outcome does not seem favorable in your life, God will never leave you nor forsake you. He will show Himself faithful every time.

The Cowardly Lion is asking for the same thing we should be desiring as descendants of the Lion of Judah, courage. Every time God calls His people to accomplish something great, He first asks them to be of good courage or to not be afraid. We see this throughout scripture.

When Joshua prepares to take the Israelites over the Jordan River and into the Promised Land, God tells him to be strong and of good courage. (Joshua 1:9)

When God is sending Jeremiah as a young prophet to the nations He tells him, *"Do not be afraid of them, for I am with you and will rescue you, declares the Lord."* (Jeremiah 1:8)

When the angels came to the shepherds to tell them of the birth of the Messiah, the angelic host said, "Fear not." (Luke 2:10)

When Timothy was about to take over the church in Ephesus after the departure of the apostle Paul, he was told that God had not given him a spirit of fear. (2 Timothy 1:7)

Every person God has called to great achievement has also been called to great audacity. The audacity to persevere through formidable frustration. The audacity to conquer that which is seemingly unconquerable. The audacity to continue moving forward through impregnable opposition. The audacity to realize your future is on the other side of your fear.

The Spirit of Fear

According to the apostle Paul in his second letter to Timothy, fear is actually a spirit. Not only is it a spirit but it is a spiritual gift. Listen to Paul as he encourages his spiritual son:

"For God hath not given us the spirit of fear; but of power, and of love, and of a sound mind." (2 Timothy 1:7 KJV)

The question then becomes, "If God did not give me this spirit of fear, how did I get it?" Fear is a spirit given to us by the enemy. Just like God gives spiritual gifts to edify and uplift the Kingdom, Satan gives spiritual gifts that tear the Kingdom down. Fear is one of Satan's weapons of mass destruction, along with guilt and accusation. It is not just an emotional manifestation of nervousness or anxiety. It is a demonic device used to frustrate the plan of God for our lives.

But just like any other gift given to you by someone you don't trust, you don't have to open it. The next time the enemy sends fear into your life, quickly respond by refusing to open it and send it back. You can't stop the devil from sending a fear package to your house, but you can refuse to receive it. Rejecting fearful thoughts by speaking and knowing the truth of God protects us from walking in fear.

When I was growing up as a minister I often heard preachers say that the phrase "Be not afraid" was in the Bible 365 times, because God knew the devil would tempt us with fear every day of the year. I don't know how theologically sound that statement is, but it sure is a relevant one. The devil knows if he can consume us with the spirit of fear our lion-like authority will never be released. In actuality, fear is not designed to annihilate the believer. It is designed to immobilize the believer.

One of the Greek words for fear is *phobos*. It is where we get the English word phobia, and its literal translation is terror or terrorism. In the last 20 years, terrorism has been at the top of every political conversation and government agenda, because of the number of lives that have been lost in the United States and countries all over the world through terrorist acts. It was on September 11, 2001 when every aspect of normality as it pertains to freedom, peace and national security changed forever.

Two commercial jetliners were used to destroy the towers of The World Trade Center in New York City, another went down directly into the Pentagon in Washington, D.C., and a fourth plane crashed in an open field in Pennsylvania. Approximately 3,000 people were killed in the most devastating terror attack in American history, and the U.S. began a "War on Terror" campaign.

It caused so much fear that governments shut down airports all over the world, people were afraid to open their own mail because of the threat of deadly chemical content and people all over the country were afraid to go to public buildings, visit the mall or even drop off letters at the local post office. For weeks, that one act of terrorism by less than 10 people shut down the most powerful country in the world.

Satan is much like al-Qaeda. He is more than a tormentor. He is a terrorist. He often causes catastrophes in our lives to create fear so we will be immobilized, unable to fulfill our divine purposes. Terrorism is always about territory. If Satan is producing fear in your life, it is an indication and a witness that God is about to take you into a new level of territory.

A Willingness to Confront our Fears

Throughout the *Wizard of Oz* story we witness the Cowardly Lion displaying subtle expressions of boldness and courage. It becomes evident to me that somewhere, beneath all of that timidity and signs of reservation and weakness there is a hint of authority within him. I'm not quite sure if the Lion's real problem is that he lacks the ability to be courageous as much as it is that he lacks a willingness to experience confrontation. It isn't that he is weak at all. He is simply afraid to confront his fears. That's the problem with many of us. We are unwilling to face our fears head on.

We all have memorized the power-packed faith scriptures of the Bible, but when it comes to applying them to our circumstances, we have difficulties.

If God be for us, He's more than the world against us. (Romans 8:31)

When the enemy comes in like a flood, God will raise up a standard against him. (Isaiah 59:19)

No weapon formed against us shall prosper and every tongue that rises up against us shall be condemned. (Isaiah 54:17)

All of these scripture are true, but not one of them will work for us without us first confronting our fears. Here's a good one that we just love. In 2 Chronicles 20, a mighty army is approaching King Jahosaphat and the people of Judah, and God says to the king,

You will not have to fight this battle. Take up your positions; stand firm and see the deliverance the Lord will give you, Judah and Jerusalem. Do not be afraid;

do not be discouraged. Go out to face them tomorrow, and the Lord will be with
you. (v. 17)

Though God tells the king he will not have to fight in the battle,
Jahosaphat still has to show up to the battleground. As a matter of fact,
God not only requires him to show up, He also instructs him to take
position, stand firm, reject fear and discouragement and face his
adversaries. It is mandatory for us all to walk through the Valley of the
Shadow of Death. We don't have to fear. We are not walking alone. God
is with us.

When I was a teenager one of my greatest fears was riding a roller
coaster. I hated even being near one. My idea of having a great time at an
amusement park involved driving the bumper cars, trying to win a stuffed
animal and eating a funnel cake or two. I was not interested in standing in
line to ride those huge roller coasters whose names alone suggested to me
that I shouldn't get on one: The Dragon Tail, The Triple Loop, The
Dungeon Dive, The Black Hole, Hell's Haven, The Monster Coaster, The
Flight of Fear. Who in their right mind would want to pay good money
and stand in line for hours to experience a ride of terror?

Naturally, all of my friends would hurtle all sorts of insults at me,
because I wouldn't ride with them. They would call me soft, weak and a
coward in hopes their insults would make me break under the pressure
and force me to ride. Not me. I've never been one to respond easily to
peer pressure.

But on one trip to the amusement park, the energy and excitement
in the voices of my friends following a roller coaster ride piqued my
curiosity. You should have seen their faces as they cheered and laughed

about how much fun they'd had. They described the dips, loops and twists so vividly I almost felt like I was on the ride with them.

I asked one of my friends a question, and his response has stuck with me to this day. "How can you get on such an obviously frightening ride without being afraid?" He responded, "Who said that I wasn't afraid? All of us are afraid of that ride. That's why we get on it."

They could ride, not because they were unafraid, but because they somehow received joy out of confronting their fear and overcoming it. In minutes I was standing in line with them, preparing myself mentally to get on this coaster. The hardest part of the process was not strapping myself in the seat belt or holding my breath as we slowly approached the highest peak of the coaster tracks. It was staying in line while waiting for my turn to approach, confronting my fear without changing my mind, that was the greatest challenge.

Isn't that it, my friends? Isn't it hard to confront the thing that has been controlling your life without yielding to the urge to shrink back and quit? The only way you can do it is to remain focused and surround yourself with people who will encourage you to stay in line. After almost 45 minutes of an internal tug of war with myself, my time to ride arrived, and I decided to strap myself in until I could barely breathe, close my eyes as tight as I could and not open them until they told me the ride was over.

But as I climbed into my seat I thought to myself, "If I close my eyes, am I really facing my fears?" My friend challenged me to consider – If I am already on the ride, and there is no turning back now, I might as well go all out and enjoy the experience. I opened my eyes, sat back in my seat and embraced the ride. I surprised myself. As I was about to go over the largest hill of the track, I bravely lifted my hands in the air, threw my head back and screamed with excitement. I can't put into words the sense of accomplishment and authority I felt. Just like the Cowardly Lion, I had tapped into an internal courage that I didn't even know was there simply by confronting my fears.

My prayer is that you might be encouraged to confront whatever fear has been haunting you and keeping you from moving deeper into your destiny. Face it. Don't retreat. Get on the ride of faith, and as God takes you over your obstacles, don't forget to lift up your hands, throw back your head and lift up your voice in victory and praise. Christ is in you, and He is the hope of glory. (Colossians 1:27)

Chapter 6

When Witches Get Worried

The Wicked Witch of the West appears in a cloud of red smoke.
"They're gone. The ruby slippers. What have you done with them?
Give them back to me."

Glenda the Good, who had come to celebrate the end of the
Wicked Witch of the East, had given the slippers to Dorothy.
"Keep tight inside of them," she says.

The Wicked Witch points a gnarled finger at Dorothy,
"I'll get you my pretty. And your little dog too."

The Wicked Witch of the West is known throughout the land of Oz as a menace, her troop of flying monkeys helping her wreak havoc in the lives of the people. The ruby slippers belonged to the Wicked Witch of the East, who was killed upon Dorothy's arrival in Oz. These are no ordinary slippers. They hold power so great that Dorothy immediately becomes the target of the Witch of the West.

The Shoes Win the Fight

A little later in this chapter we will talk about how God gives us His Spirit as a weapon against our enemy. He also gives us the Word to accompany it. *"The Spirit gives life; the flesh counts for nothing. The words I have spoken to you— they are full of the Spirit and life."* (John 6:63)

At the very end of our story, Dorothy and her friends are trapped in the witch's castle. They have nowhere to run or hide and have seemingly come to the end of their journey. This is when the witch makes a request that she's made throughout the story, yet I somehow missed. She didn't ask for Dorothy's life. She asked for Dorothy's shoes. This whole time the witch was never really after Dorothy. She just wanted what was on her feet.

What if I were to tell you that Satan has never really been after you, but he is really after your feet, which represent the Word of God? Satan knows we are both powerless and defenseless without the Word of God, so he attacks us in any way possible to steal the truth from us. A passage in Luke 4 illustrates how powerful the Word can be when used as a weapon against Satan.

> *Jesus, full of the Holy Spirit, left the Jordan and was led by the Spirit into the wilderness, where for forty days he was tempted by the devil. He ate nothing during those days, and at the end of them he was hungry. The devil said to him, "If you are the Son of God, tell this stone to become bread." Jesus answered, "It is written: 'Man shall not live on bread alone.'" The devil led him up to a high place and showed him in an instant all the kingdoms of the world. And he said to him, "I will give you all their authority and splendor; it has been given to me, and I can give it to anyone I want to. If you worship me, it will all be yours." Jesus answered, "It is written: 'Worship the Lord your God and serve him only.'"*

The devil led him to Jerusalem and had him stand on the highest point of the temple. "If you are the Son of God," he said, "throw yourself down from here. For it is written: "He will command his angels concerning you to guard you carefully; they will lift you up in their hands, so that you will not strike your foot against a stone."" Jesus answered, "It is said: 'Do not put the Lord your God to the test.'" When the devil had finished all this tempting, he left him until an opportune time. (v. 1-13)

Satan attacks Jesus at one of the weakest times of His life, after 40 days of fasting. He doesn't attack Him in the temple or in one of the synagogues but corners Him in the wilderness. He repeatedly tempts Jesus to get out of the will of His Father and to abort His destiny. First he tempts Jesus to turn a stone into bread to appease His flesh. Then he tempts Jesus to jump from a high place and commit suicide. Then he tempts Jesus to abandon His faith and bow down and worship him.

With every tactical scheme and crafty trick, Jesus defeats Satan without fail. How? By using the Word of God as His weapon of mass destruction. Every time the devil attacks Jesus, Jesus counters the attack with, *"It is written..."*, quoting the Word of God and proclaiming truth. If we are going to overcome our temptations and have victory over Satan, sin and, even sometimes, ourselves we are going to have to use our "shoes," the Word, as our weapon.

Several years ago, when my daughter was about five, our church was worshipping on a college campus. After service, all of the kids went outside to play. A few minutes later I heard a loud scream. My daughter had been stung on the nose by a bee while playing outside with the other kids. I immediately began to comfort her, and asked her if any of the other kids had been stung.

She said, "No daddy. That bee only wanted to sting me." She said the bee picked her out, because he didn't like her. I assured her the bee was not just picking on her. She was just the one with the bad luck that day. As I pulled her closer to me to kiss her nose, I smelled a distinct sweet smell, the bubble gum in her mouth. It all began to make sense. The bee that stung her smelled the same sweet smell I had. It was not after my daughter but what was in her mouth.

The attacks that you are experiencing are not always about what you are doing wrong or even what you haven't done right. They could simply be a result of the Word that God has placed in your mouth. Family, whatever you do, don't give up your shoes. Don't stop relying on the Word of God to be your final source of authority. Don't allow your circumstances to become so overwhelming that they distract you from the promises of God that have been spoken over your life. And don't allow the enemy to sweet talk you into believing he can usher you into a blessed place barefoot. Heaven and Earth shall pass away but God's Word will last forever.

The Shoes Build Your Faith

Throughout the story, Dorothy encouraged herself by singing what I like to call her destiny anthem,

Follow the yellow brick road
Follow, follow, follow, follow, follow the yellow brick road

We're off to see the wizard, the wonderful Wizard of Oz

We hear he is a whiz of a wiz

If ever a wiz there was

The Wizard of Oz is one because, because, because,

because, because, because, because of the wonderful things he does

We're off to see the wizard the wonderful Wizard of Oz

Dorothy is on a mission to meet the powerful wizard. We'll soon see that she is looking to the wrong source for what she needs, but even so, she was definitely going about it the right way. She knew that if she was going to reach her destiny without giving up along the way, she would have to constantly speak it out of her mouth.

Dorothy revitalizes her faith by singing her anthem of encouragement, "Follow the Yellow Brick Road." Not only does she sing this song of destiny, faith and promise but she encourages every person she runs into to sing the song as well. By the time Dorothy arrives at the Emerald City, she's got the Scarecrow, Tin Man and Cowardly Lion singing. Toto would probably have tried to sing a line or two if he had the ability to speak. If you're honest, you have probably been humming along with the melody as well.

Faith-filled, encouraging words are contagious and critical to our success. Speaking the Word of God leads you to the promises of God. You are today what you said about yourself yesterday and you will be tomorrow what you say about yourself today. That's why it's so important to speak the promises of God over yourself, over your family and over your future daily. *"So then faith cometh by hearing, and hearing by the word of God."* (Romans 10:17 KJV)

But Dorothy's victory does not just come about because of what she says. It's also a result of what she does. She's not just singing about what she desires to have happen in her life. She is also taking steps forward to make it happen.

I've been in full time church ministry for almost 24 years, and if I have learned anything, I've learned how to have church. I know how to dress on Sundays. I know what places during the service to stand up and sit down. I know when to clap and when to bow my head in serenity. I know when to say "amen" and when to sing with the choir. All of that stuff is the easy part. The challenge is walking it out after the benediction is given. I believe that's why the scriptures often compare the Word of God to our feet.

> *Thy **Word** is a lamp unto my **FEET** and a light unto my path.* (Psalm 119:105 KJV)

> *Therefore put on the full armor of God, so that when the day of evil comes, you may be able to stand your ground, and after you have done everything, to stand. Stand firm then, with the belt of truth buckled around your waist, with the breastplate of righteousness in place, and with your **FEET** fitted with the readiness that comes from the **gospel** of peace.* (Ephesians 6:13-15)

> *How, then, can they call on the one they have not believed in? And how can they believe in the one of whom they have not heard? And how can they hear without someone preaching to them? And how can anyone **preach** unless they are sent?*

*As it is written: "How beautiful are the **FEET** of those who bring good news!"* (Romans 10:14-15)

In these passages, God intentionally uses the image of **feet** to illustrate His Word. Why? Because the Word only works after it has worked its way down from our mouths to our feet.

The Word will never work for us if we just continue to sing about it on the yellow brick road of life. It has to eventually be walked out if it's going to make a difference in and through us.

It's alright to sing about God's amazing grace, but eventually we have to extend it to others when we have been offended.

It's wonderful to sing "Pass Me Not, Oh Gentle Savior," but we can't continue passing up people who are desperately in need of our assistance.

It's great to sing the old hymn "Victory Is Mine," but sooner or later we must use the gifts and talents God has given us in order to obtain that victory.

Talk is cheap. Destiny is discovered for Dorothy when she clicks her heels together and says, "There's no place like home." Destiny will be discovered for us when we use our mouths and our feet together to do the will of the Father.

Bring Me the Broom

When Dorothy and her friends reach the Emerald City, the gatekeeper refuses to allow them in. Can you image how they felt to get that close to where they'd been dreaming to be for days and yet be denied access? They had endured the difficulties of the journey, the danger of the forest, the threats of the wicked witch and even a near death experience in the poppy field, and now they find themselves standing behind a closed door. Dorothy pleads with the gatekeeper who refuses access until she makes one statement: Glenda the Good sent me.

When asked for proof, Dorothy shows the gatekeeper the ruby slippers. Remember earlier I told you the shoes represent the Word of God. It is the Word of God that gives us access to doors that have been shut in our faces. It is the apostle John in Revelation who says, *"Behold, I have set before thee an open door, and no man can shut it."* (Revelation 3:8)

Dorothy and her friends enter the city and are eventually left at the door of the wizard's chambers. They walk up a long, royal corridor and enter a vast room filled with large billows of smoke and blazing flames of fire. The voice of the wizard sounds like thunder roaring from Heaven. It is both awesome and awful at the same time. As they walk closer to the sound of the voice they begin to state their requests. The Lion pleads his case for courage, the Scarecrow shares what he'd do if he only had a brain, the Tin Man nervously asks for a beating heart and, with tears in her eyes, Dorothy begs the wizard to show her the way home.

To their surprise, the wizard responds favorably, promising to use his power to give them everything they desire. But it is all contingent on one thing: The witch's broom. He has the audacity to ask them to bring him the witch's broom before he grants their requests.

This is an impossible thing to ask. In order to bring the witch's broom, they must first overthrow the witch. But maybe the wizard is onto something. Maybe it is the removal of the witch's broom that gives them power over the witch. What does the witch use her broom for anyway? It transports her from place to place so she may work out all her wicked schemes. The broom is what the witch rides on.

There is a parallel here for the life of the believer. If I can take away what the devil is riding on in my life to lead me to sin and destruction, I can rob him of all of his power. Be honest with yourself for a moment. What are you allowing the enemy to ride on in your life? In what areas of your life are you allowing the enemy to have access? How are you opening the door for him to enter into your life and heart and wreak havoc?

Is it your unforgiveness and bitterness, your fear and low self-esteem, your lust and sensuality, your anger and bitterness, your bigotry and racism, your pride, your arrogance, your greed? What is the broom of temptation the enemy has been riding on in your life for years that continues to keep you from walking into your purpose?

Until you can openly and honestly answer that question, you will never be able to overcome your struggles and realize your potential. You can't kill your witch until you take her broom.

Not only do we have to identify our brooms of weakness and temptation, we also have to get rid of them. How do I get rid of the thing that the enemy has been riding on in my life for years? We bring the broom to God. It is Jesus who said in Matthew 11:28-30,

> *Are you tired? Worn out? Burned out on religion? Come to me. Get away with me and you'll recover your life. I'll show you how to take a real rest. Walk with me and work with me—watch how I do it. Learn the unforced rhythms of grace. I won't lay anything heavy or ill-fitting on you. Keep company with me and you'll learn to live freely and lightly. (MSG)*

The Master is challenging us to bring our brooms home, to carry to Him all of our secrets, inadequacies, shortcomings and temptations and just rest in Him. If you bring Him your broom, He will take care of your witch.

> *No test or temptation that comes your way is beyond the course of what others have had to face. All you need to remember is that God will never let you down; he'll never let you be pushed past your limit; he'll always be there to help you come through it.* (1 Corinthians 10:13 MSG)

The Witch, the Weapons and the Water

While on their way to retrieve the witch's broom, Dorothy and her friends are attacked by the wicked witch's flying monkeys. They capture Dorothy and Toto and carry them back to the witch's castle. The Scarecrow, Tin Man and Cowardly Lion take off in pursuit of Dorothy and Toto, devising a plan to rescue their friends.

The rescue crew is able to enter the witch's compound, locate Dorothy and Toto, and hightail it out of the witch's castle. But it doesn't take long for the witch's guards to track them down and surround them, trapping them in a high tower. After all they've done to get to this point, it seems they have come to the end of their journey. There is no way they can escape this time. The witch begins to hurl threats and insults at Dorothy and her friends in hopes of emotionally terrorizing them before she actually destroys them.

That's a great tool of Satan. He overwhelms us with so much fear, we submit to his will for our lives and forfeit all that God has in store for us. The witch begins to descriptively talk about the horrible things she's going to do to each of Dorothy's friends, and turning to the Scarecrow, takes the base of her broom, ignites it with a nearby lantern and ruthlessly sets the Scarecrow's straw on fire.

In both panic and compassion, Dorothy reaches down and grabs a bucket of water, throwing it toward the Scarecrow in an attempt to save him. But the water doesn't just drench the Scarecrow. It also drenches the witch. The witch begins to scream in agony and torment, "I'm melting! I'm melting!" She begins to shrink until she completely disappears into a pile of old, battered clothes. Nothing is left of her but her smoldering black dress, her singed witch's hat and her useless broom. Dorothy kills the greatest threat in the land of Oz with a bucket of water. This is how you destroy your witch. In John 7:37-39 we read,

> On the last and greatest day of the festival, Jesus stood and said in a loud voice, "Let anyone who is thirsty come to me and drink. Whoever believes in me, as Scripture has said, **rivers of living water** will flow from within them." **By this he meant the Spirit,** whom those who believed in him were later to receive. Up to that time the Spirit had not been given, since Jesus had not yet been glorified.

God has given you the Spirit to destroy every enemy that stands in between you and your destiny. Nothing can stand against the Spirit of God. Zechariah 4:6 says that it is "'not by might nor by power, but by my Spirit,' says the Lord Almighty." You are too weak to fight the witch yourself. You are too small to defeat such a big problem on your own. But when you yield yourself to the power of God, bringing your brooms to him and allowing His Spirit to fight for you, you cannot lose.

Daryl W. Arnold

Notice that when Dorothy's friends come to destroy the witch and complete their rescue mission, they come with carnal weapons. The Scarecrow comes with a gun, the Tin Man with a rusty ax and the Cowardly Lion with a butterfly net. How silly it is for them to try to defeat such a powerful witch with such menial weapons. It is equally as silly when we try to defeat our adversary on our own with fleshly weapons. You don't need carnal weapons. You need Spiritual Water. You need to be filled with the Spirit of God and allow Him to fight your battles for you.

Did you notice that Dorothy's aim was never to kill the witch with the bucket of water? It was an accident. Dorothy was really trying to save the Scarecrow from being consumed by the fire of the witch. But as it turns out, the same water that was used to save the Scarecrow's life was the same water that ended up killing the witch. In the same way, it is critical for us as believers to completely depend upon the Spirit who both gives us abundant life and protects us from the attacks of our antagonizer.

The same Spirit who energizes us to achieve our divine endeavors is the same Spirit who has the power to destroy anything that would seek to deter us. My brothers and sisters, live by the Spirit, rest in the Spirit, be led by the Spirit, be filled with the Spirit and be consumed by the Spirit. Receive by faith the promises of Jesus In John 4.

Jesus answered, "Everyone who drinks this water will be thirsty again, but whoever drinks the water I give them will never thirst. Indeed, the water I give them will become in them a spring of water welling up to eternal life." (v. 13-14)

Chapter 7

The Wizard's Weakness

"We're off to see the Wizard
The wonderful Wizard of Oz
We hear he is a whiz of a wiz
If ever a wiz there was
If ever, oh, ever a wiz there was
The Wizard of Oz is one because
of the wonderful things he does."

The entire narrative of the *Wizard of Oz* is centered around the wizard's ability to meet the needs of every other character in the story. Everyone Dorothy meets suggests if there's any hope at all for Dorothy and her three friends, it can be found only through the powers of the great Wizard of Oz.

Over half of the movie focuses on the journey to the Emerald City just to be in his presence. It is obvious to all of us that the Wizard has to represent God in the narrative, right? Only God can give a heart to the heartless, a mind to those who have lost it, courage and power to the fearful and direction to those who have lost their way. The wizard has to represent God.

Let's not jump to that conclusion so quickly. As we saw in the earlier chapter, Dorothy and her friends go to the witch's castle, destroy the witch and retrieve her broom. They return to the wizard, giving him what he asked so he can in turn give them what he promised. But when they arrive, they receive a great disappointment. The wizard breaks his promise, telling them to come back another day. They had been through so much to heed his requests, and it was all in vain.

As Dorothy pleads with the wizard to reconsider, Toto runs through the thick, black smoke and the flashing lights and pulls back an emerald green curtain, revealing a small man pulling levers, pushing buttons and yelling into an old microphone. The powerful Wizard of Oz, the one everyone believed could do great and wonderful things, isn't so powerful after all. He is merely a man with a machine pretending to be something he is not and, worst of all, making promises he never had the ability to fulfill.

You see, family, the Wizard of Oz does not represent God; he actually represents religion, and there is a huge difference between the two. Religion is a manmade set of systems, rules and regulations based upon do's and don'ts in life. It promises that if you just go to church every week – on the correct day, of course – pay your tithes, dress in the appropriate attire, talk like everybody else in the club and look the part, you will be rewarded with the promises of God. Religion encourages us to stay in the box of traditionalism and to not ask questions about who is behind the curtains. Religion is designed to keep us chasing after something we can never receive without the help of God.

God has never been an advocate for religion. As a matter of fact, he's always been an enemy of it. It was Jesus who said in Mark 7:13, *"Thus you nullify the word of God by your tradition that you have handed down. And you do many things like that."* You can care more about your laws, ordinances and traditions than people themselves. In John 5, Jesus healed a man who had been a cripple for 38 years. He was not able to walk his son to school, work and provide for his wife and family, or accompany his daughter down the aisle and give her away in marriage. He was a broken, battered, begging invalid who had to daily depend on the assistance of others. One day, he has an encounter with Jesus. The Master heals this man completely and tells him to pick up the mat he was lying on and move into his bright future.

The first place he goes is the temple, a place he just knew he would be encouraged and celebrated. Instead of receiving rejoicing, he receives rebuke, not because he was healed but because he had been healed on the wrong day, the Sabbath. (John 5:1-16) Isn't that just ridiculous? Shouldn't everyone have been excited about what God had done for this man? But that's not how religion works. It cares more about keeping the rules of man than cultivating a relationship with God, all the while, making promises it can never keep.

When the Lord first started compelling me to come to Him and challenged me to completely yield to His lordship, I rebelled, not because I didn't believe in God or questioned His existence but because I didn't think I could meet His standards. I didn't want to be a hypocrite, so I told the Lord I would come to Him when I cleaned myself up.

What I didn't know is that you can't clean a fish until you catch him. I didn't realize that God loved me just like I was, and if I were to ever be cleaned up, He would have to do the cleaning. I couldn't distinguish the difference between having religion and having a relationship. But when I stopped running and surrendered my heart to Him instead of the machine behind the curtain, I found out that everything I ever needed, wanted or even imagined was all in Him. What was even more exciting was His life inside of me. In Him do we live, in Him do we move and in Him do we have our being. (Acts 17:28)

My friend, just as the wizard was an enormous disappointment to Dorothy because He promised her something he could not give her, religion, with its manmade rules and regulations, will also be a great disappointment to you, because following the rules cannot give you what can only be found in God who lives in you. I pastor one of the most amazing churches in the world. The people love me and my family and earnestly believe in the vision.

But I notice they sometimes seem to have more faith in me than in the One who sent me. I often remind them that I may be a man of God, but I am not the god of man. Pastors and minister are merely tools in the hands of a holy God, designed to build His Kingdom. You will never find destiny in pastors, popes, bishops, denominations or any human entity on Earth. It is only in His presence that we have the fullness of joy.

Chapter 8

A Message from Man's Best Friend

When the Wicked Witch of the West turns her back, Toto leaps up and out of the room where he and Dorothy are being held. He runs from the castle, back through the dark forest and finds the Tin Man, Scarecrow and Cowardly Lion.

"Look! There's Toto. Where'd he come from?" the Tin Man asks.

"Don't you see," says the Scarecrow, "He's come to take us to Dorothy."

Toto leads Dorothy's friends back to the witch's castle to rescue her.

To be perfectly honest, this chapter wasn't originally supposed to be in the book. It was a last minute addendum added a week before the book was sent to editing. Who writes an entire chapter about an old, 13-pound Cairn Terrier who doesn't have a single line in our story? But the closer I came to finishing the manuscript, the more I felt I was leaving out something really important. You know that feeling you get when you're on your way to work or leaving on a vacation, and you just know in your gut you were about to leave something behind you would regret later? That's the feeling I kept getting. What was I leaving out that was so important that it wouldn't let me sleep at night?

It was Toto. He was the missing piece. I realize that Toto isn't the main character of the story, but his role in Dorothy's journey is incredibly significant. If he isn't anything else, he is one heck of a friend. Toto is the only character in the story who is there for Dorothy from the beginning to the end.

I don't know if people really comprehend the value found in a friend or a genuine relationship these days. Friendship has sadly been reduced to how many followers you have on Twitter or how many likes and shares you have on Facebook. That's not real friendship at all. Friendships are not just haphazard relationships that develop by coincidence while walking down the path of life. Friendships are bonds formed through divine providence. They are necessary for one to accomplish their God-given destiny.

Whether we appreciate it or not, God created us to be social beings, and He masterfully designed us to depend on one another. Listen to the apostle Paul as he shares a word picture of how God has created his people to work together in union.

> *Then we will no longer be infants, tossed back and forth by the waves, and blown here and there by every wind of teaching and by the cunning and craftiness of people in their deceitful scheming. Instead, speaking the truth in love, we will grow to become in every respect the mature body of him who is the head, that is, Christ. From him the whole body, joined and held together by every supporting ligament, grows and builds itself up in love, as each part does its work.* (Ephesians 4:14-16)

There are two words that jump out at me when reading that scripture, **together** and **love**. Friendship is growing TOGETHER, IN LOVE, regardless of what life's circumstances may be. We see this powerfully displayed through Toto and Dorothy's relationship. They have a love for one another in the beginning of the story, while in the comfort of Kansas, but also while in the dark shadows of the wicked witch's castle at the end of the journey. Now, that's real friendship.

Bishop T. D. Jakes, a well-known African American pastor, movie producer and author, stated something years ago in one of his sermons that I've never forgotten. He said that God places people in your life for one of three purposes: a reason, a season or a lifetime. It is our job to make sure that we put them in the right category. His argument is that we oftentimes try to take *reason* and *season* people, who are meant to be part of our lives temporarily, and make them *lifetime* people, and we get frustrated when they leave.

In this particular story Glenda the Good was a *reason* person to Dorothy. She was only in Dorothy's life to point her in the right direction. The Scarecrow, the Tin Man and the Lion were *season* people. They were only in one another's lives to help each other receive what they thought they were missing. But Toto was a *lifetime* friend. He was in Dorothy's life forever. Our challenge is to seek God and ask who is supposed to be in our lives in a significant way and for how long.

I truly believe that success and failure are strongly determined by the company you keep. When I think about the greatest seasons of failure I've had, I can generally trace them back to a time I was keeping company with the wrong people. I've learned that whoever has my ear and my eye generally has my heart. I am a firm believer that we are the sum total of what we set our affections on, and we eventually become that which we behold. We will ultimately reflect the image of those who have captured our attention. Maybe that's why the Bible says we should lay aside every sin and weight that so easily besets us, looking unto Jesus the author and finisher of our faith. (Hebrews 12:1) We cannot lay aside our sin and weight unless we behold Jesus. We become what we behold. Naturally, the enemy strategically places negative people in our lives to deter and delay us from our destiny.

On the other hand, when I think of the greatest successes I've had in life, they are also attributed to the positive role models and mentors the Lord gave me in that season. From my mother who taught me I could overcome any obstacle placed in front of me and could become more than my past environment, to my first Pastor Rev. H. H. Wright who taught me that true Kingdom ministry is so much more than simply mastering the art of hermeneutics and homiletics, but involves healing the hurts of the least and the lost. To Bishop Kevin Adams who taught me the importance of being biblically sound, studying to show myself approved and to maintain theological integrity when teaching God's people. To my wife who constantly teaches me that at the end of our lives all we will really have left is our faith and our family. I pray that God would give you a Toto and that when He does, you will recognize and honor that gift. And I pray you would be a Toto for others, the tool God uses to help build someone else's destiny.

The Silent Partner

As I mentioned, Toto plays a tremendous role in Dorothy's journey but he never speaks a word. One of the things that took me many years to learn as a pastor is that I don't always have to have the correct answer, or even have to say anything at all, when people are hurting. I often had this overwhelming feeling of guilt and failure when one of my parishioners had a tragedy hit their lives and I didn't have the words to explain it away – an innocent child being killed in a drive by shooting, a baby being born with a brain tumor, a faithful wife finding out that her husband of years was having an affair. God had to teach me that sometimes people don't need your perspective. They only need your presence. That's what Toto was for Dorothy, present.

There's a story told about a little boy who asked his mother if he could go outside and ride bikes with his friend, Timmy. His mother told him he could as long as he was home before the street lights came on. After several hours go by, the mother realized it was getting late and she hadn't heard from her son. A few minutes later, the street lights came on and he was still not there. After another hour of mixed emotions, feeling angry, dishonored and increasingly afraid, she considered calling the police.

Just as she was about to call, she heard her son coming through the door and angrily said, "Where have you been? I've been worried sick about you." He responded saying someone had stolen Timmy's bike while they were in the convenience store, and they had been out looking for it.

"Well did you find it?"

"No ma'am we didn't."

"Then what have you been doing all of these hours?"

"I just sat down on the curb and cried with Timmy until he was strong enough to go home."

A friend doesn't always have the answers when life steals something precious from you, but a real friend will sit on the curb and cry with you until you become stronger.

Those of us who are strong and able in the faith need to step in and lend a hand to those who falter, and not just do what is most convenient for us. Strength is for service, not status. Each one of us needs to look after the good of the people around us, asking ourselves, "How can I help?" That's exactly what Jesus did. He didn't make it easy for himself by avoiding people's troubles, but waded right in and helped out. (Romans 15:1-3 MSG)

Scene after scene, we notice that everywhere Dorothy goes, her best friend Toto is right there, standing by her side. Proverbs 17:17 says, *"A friend loves at all times, and a brother is born for a time of adversity."* If friendships are going to be authentic, they must be built on the foundation of honesty. Just because a friend stands with you doesn't mean they have to agree with you. I often tell people that a real friend will allow you to rest while you're dreaming, but will wake you up when you're having a nightmare.

Those are the types of people I want in my life, people who will not only protect me from others but will even protect me from myself. I need people who will encourage me to accomplish my dreams and endeavors without being envious, but I also want a friend who will wake me up when I am making destructive decisions that could ultimately turn my destiny into a nightmare.

Dorothy and Toto's friendship is marked by sacrifice and altruism. On multiple occasions we witness Dorothy and all of her friends sacrificing themselves for the welfare of others. One of the most memorable statements Jesus made in His life is found in John 15:13, *"Greater love has no one than this: to lay down one's life for one's friends."* That one verse characterized His entire purpose for coming to Earth, to lay down His life for His friends and to challenge us to do the same for others, maybe not in a literal way but to esteem others more highly than ourselves.

Several years ago I was watching a documentary about Ross McGinnis, a man who received the Medal of Honor, one of the highest military awards given by the President of the United States. He was a private in the U.S. Army and wanted to be a soldier since kindergarten. When he was 19, his unit was deployed to Baghdad where he was assigned as a machine gunner. On December 4, his platoon was attacked and a grenade was thrown into his vehicle.

He warned his four friends to take cover and selflessly threw himself on the blast, losing his life but saving his friends. A reporter asked one of the survivors what his initial response was to the attack. The soldier said he took cover until it was safe. When he looked down at himself, he noticed he was covered with blood from his head to his boots. He said he just knew he was dying. But after the smoke cleared, he realized it wasn't his own blood covering him but the blood of his friend who had just given his own life to save him. What an amazing comparison to how Jesus threw Himself on our sins and selflessly gave up His life by covering us with His own blood. Destiny can only be accomplished when there are people in our lives who will selflessly cover us until we fulfill our purpose and callings.

Chapter 9

Don't Miss Your Destiny

With the Wizard powerless to provide her with a way to return home, Dorothy asks Glenda the Good to come to her aid.

"You've always had the power to go back to Kansas," Glenda says.

"Then why didn't you tell her before?" asks the Scarecrow.

"Because she wouldn't have believed me. She had to learn it for herself."

"Well," Dorothy says, "If I ever go looking for my heart's desire again, I won't look any further than my own backyard, because if it isn't there, I never really lost it to begin with."

What have you been pursuing? What has been occupying your time and attention? What is it that you, in thought and deed, believe is the key to the life you've wanted, to filling the deep void inside of you?

At the beginning of her journey, Dorothy wanted out of Kansas. She believed it was in a place far away that she would receive the great things she deeply desired. It was then that her dreams would become a reality and her troubles would fade away. It's only after she survives a terrible storm, enters new territory and purses a wizard who she thought would meet her needs but ultimately fails her that she realizes all she has ever really desired can be found inside of herself.

Dorothy isn't alone. The same is true for you and for me. In the first few pages of this book, I said that God created us with a hole inside, an eternal vacuum that demands to be filled. Like Dorothy, we attempt to satisfy that longing with the temporal things of this world – money, sex, prestige, drugs, acceptance – but have found time and again that these things are insufficient.

The longing within you isn't a bad thing, nor is it an accident. You wouldn't have this desire for more if it couldn't be fulfilled. It is part of each of us by design. I believe God has created us with this void, so we will come to Him to be completed. Throughout His Word, God extends an invitation to us to receive Him and be satisfied.

When he says, *"Come all who are thirsty, come to the waters; and you who have no money, come, buy and eat!"* he is speaking to those of us who are spiritually thirsty, who have tried and failed to be satisfied by the temporal trappings of this world. (Isaiah 55:1)

In John 6, Jesus takes just five loaves and two small fish and multiplies them to feed five thousand people. It is a miraculous expression of provision and power. Jesus later encourages his disciples:

Do not work for food that spoils, but for food that endures to eternal life, which the Son of Man will give you...I am the bread of life. Whoever comes to me will never go hungry, and whoever believes in me will never be thirsty. But as I told you, you have seen me and still you do not believe. All those the Father gives me will come to me, and whoever comes to me I will never drive away. (v. 35-37)

It is He and He alone who can bring us joy and ultimate peace. In His presence is the fullness of joy, and only in Him can you receive peace that passes all understanding. You cannot find satisfaction in a nightclub, in a penthouse suite, in the back of a stretch limousine, nor in an executive corner office of a skyscraper complex. You can't even find it in the four walls of a brick and mortar church building. It can only be found in Him. For in Him do you live. In Him do you move. In Him do you have your being. (Acts 17:28)

King David knew this well. He experienced his own treacherous life journey. He conquered giants, survived harrowing battles, built a magnificent kingdom and brought prosperity to God's people. He also made his share of grave mistakes – Just read 2 Samuel 11. He, like us, strayed from the yellow brick road, abandoning the plans God had for him. But David always returned to what he knew to be true, saying in Psalm 16, *"You, Lord, are all I have, and you give me all I need; my future is in your hands."* (v. 5 GNT) David knew his destiny was found in obedience to God.

Look No Further

Throughout his ministry, Jesus called on all people to *"Repent, for the kingdom of God is at hand."* (Matthew 3:2) With his coming to Earth, willingness to die on a cross and his triumphant resurrection, Christ not only made a way for us to connect with God directly but for God, by the Spirit, to live inside each of us. If you have come to the saving knowledge of Jesus Christ, you are now a temple of the Lord, possessing his presence and power. The destiny you seek, the purpose you crave, is already inside of you.

What Dorothy's adventure teaches us is that there is no particular circumstance that will lead us to what we desire. She isn't the only one who discovers this. The Scarecrow insists he doesn't have a brain, the Tin Man is convinced he has no heart and the Cowardly Lion is confident he lacks courage, but throughout the story, their actions prove they already have what they believe is missing. This is most clear when they pursue the Wicked Witch's flying monkeys who have captured Dorothy. If you pay attention to the story you'll see –

It is the brainless Scarecrow who develops a strategy for freeing Dorothy.

It is the heartless Tin Man who convinces the others it's the right thing to do.

It's the cowardly Lion who leads the pursuit into the witch's castle.

It's not that these three characters lacked courage, heart and brains. They simply failed to see and live into what they already possessed. What about you? I would wager there is evidence of your God-given destiny at work in your life. Are you living as though it is up to you to find the person, place, job or circumstance that will finally give you purpose and life? Do not ignore what is already in you. Our destiny is realized when we seek the Lord and follow the plans he has for us in obedience.

Enjoying the Journey

There's one final lesson I think Dorothy can teach us. Earlier we talked about Dorothy's anthem of destiny, the song she sings throughout her journey. If you've seen the movie, you know that every time she meets a new friend, and through each step she takes, Dorothy does so with joy. Despite the fact that she is lost, an evil witch is at her heels and there is no guarantee of a way home, she enjoys the journey along the way.

Our pursuit down the yellow brick road, the plan God has for us, will take a lifetime. I have lived a handful of decades myself, have served in ministry for more than 20 years and travel the world proclaiming this good news, and I still haven't arrived. But I've learned that every day I wake up with God's purpose on my mind and the passion in my heart to fulfill it, I'm in the will of God. The journey is all a part of the plan of God.

We all know that the ultimate purpose for Jesus coming to Earth was to redeem mankind from his sins and reconcile him to God. But the process was a part of the plan. God could have easily created Jesus as a fully grown man and had Him die and be resurrected on the same day but He didn't. He allowed Him to be born as a baby, just like us. To grow up under the authority of human parents, just like us. To struggle with the temptations of this world, just like us. To be betrayed and denied by friends and family who He loved dearly, just like us. To be celebrated by some and to be crucified by others, just like us. He did all of this so that He could identify with the ups and downs of life as a human being. And every step of the way He fully embraces the journey. He knew that it was all connected to His Father's sovereign will and He learned to the enjoy the process on His way to the promise.

That is my prayer for you. *"That in all of your getting you will get understanding."* (Proverbs 4:7 KJV) That you will understand God has given you everything you need in order for you to accomplish your goals. That you would understand Christ is living inside of you and is giving you an eternal hope of glory beyond your wildest imagination. That you would understand that if your destiny is to be discovered at all, then it must be discovered from within. That you would understand that no weapon that is formed against you will ever prosper, and the Father's best for you is your only option. I look forward to your future. Welcome home!

There's No Place Like Home

Discovering the Destiny Within

Study Guide

How to Use This Study Guide

It is easy to read through a book, highlight a few phrases and put it down, quickly forgetting what was written in its pages. This study guide is designed to help you not only read scripture and encounter truth but to encourage a deeper understanding of the things of God that have the potential to change your life.

This study guide can be used for individual or group reflection.

In the following pages you will find purposeful and pragmatic questions designed to provoke reflection. As you work through the pages...

Begin with prayer, asking God to lead and guide your reflection.

Be intentional and honest in your answers. Nothing inhibits growth like denial can. Courageously answer each question truthfully.

Feel free to reference the content of the corresponding chapter. Each portion of the book in the previous pages provides important context for the questions in the study guide. Be encouraged to flip back and forth.

Complete the Destiny Prayer at the conclusion of each set of questions. At the end of each set of questions, there is ample space provided for you to conclude your reflection with prayer.

There is no formula for that time of prayer, but you may consider beginning with worship and thanksgiving to God for revealing to you His Word concerning your purpose. You might ask the Father to help you to step into obedience and make choices that will lead you toward joyful fulfillment of every destiny assignment He has for you. Finally, I encourage you to ask the Father to give you the oil of the Spirit so you might persevere on the journey He has marked out for you.

May God bless the time you spend in prayer and reflection.

Chapter 1: The Diaries of Dorothy (Page 9)

Describe a time in your journey when you felt as though there was void or emptiness in your life.

_____

_____

_____

_____

_____

_____

_____

What are some of the things you tried to fill that void with outside of God?

_____

_____

_____

_____

_____

_____

_____

Stormproof (Page 10)

How do you typically respond when you experience an unexpected storm, when things in your life may feel like they are falling apart or simply will not go your way?

_____

_____

_____

_____

_____

_____

_____

As you think back on your life, what are some storms you have experienced that you thought would destroy you yet ultimately pushed you towards your destiny?

_____

_____

_____

_____

_____

_____

_____

Having read this chapter, how can you respond differently when facing difficult circumstances in life?

_____

_____

_____

_____

_____

_____

_____

_____

If He Did it Before, He Will Do it Again (Page 13)
One of Satan's greatest strategies is to try to convince us that God will abandon us in our time of despair. Identify a time when Satan convinced you that God had forsaken you.

_____

_____

_____

_____

_____

_____

_____

_____

Describe a time when you were facing hardships, and God came to your aid.

_____

_____

_____

_____

_____

_____

_____

_____

Is it difficult for you to trust God, even after He has shown Himself to be faithful to you in the past? Why do you think that is?

_____

_____

_____

_____

_____

_____

_____

_____

How will you use what you have learned from this chapter to deepen your trust in God and His faithfulness in the future?

_____

_____

_____

_____

_____

_____

_____

Public Intoxication (Page 15)
Are you sometimes too worried about how people perceive you? Whose opinion of you matters most to you?

_____

_____

_____

_____

_____

_____

_____

_____

How have you been personally affected by your attempts to measure your worth and sense of self by the opinions of others?

_____

_____

_____

_____

_____

_____

_____

What have you learned in this chapter that may help you escape this unnecessary pressure?

_____

_____

_____

_____

_____

_____

_____

My Destiny Prayer

Take a moment to conclude your time of reflection with prayer in the space provided.

_____

_____

_____

_____

_____

_____

_____

_____

_____

_____

_____

_____

_____

_____

_____

_____

_____

Chapter 2: **Follow the Yellow Brick Road** (Page 18)

This chapter talks about the importance of discovering God's purpose for our lives and how to follow His plan that we might accomplish it. Have you ever considered God's ultimate reason for why you were born and how he might have you impact the world?

_____

_____

_____

_____

_____

_____

_____

Have you ever wrestled with the notion that you were merely one drop in the ocean of life and that your existence really didn't make much of a difference? How does it make you feel when you hear that God intentionally created you to accomplish His will on the earth?

_____

_____

_____

_____

_____

_____

Although God has a great plan for our lives, it can only come to fruition through our obedience. What are some of the shortcuts the enemy has tempted you to take in an attempt to get you off course?

_____

_____

_____

_____

_____

_____

_____

What was the cost and the consequence you had to pay for taking shortcuts in life? How far would you be in your success if you would have simply stayed on God's path?

_____

_____

_____

_____

_____

_____

_____

_____

Even when we choose to take shortcuts, God's mercy makes a way for another chance. Describe a time when God rescued you from a destructive decision and started a new season in your life.

_____

_____

_____

_____

_____

_____

_____

It's important to take the time to not only thank God for new seasons, but to protect ourselves from similar situations in the future. How will you position yourself in a way that prevents you from returning to the habit of choosing life's shortcuts?

_____

_____

_____

_____

_____

_____

_____

What are some ways you can discourage others on the journey from taking the same shortcuts you have taken?

_____

_____

_____

_____

_____

_____

_____

What was the most significant lesson you learned from this portion of the chapter? How will you apply it to your life?

_____

_____

_____

_____

_____

_____

_____

My Destiny Prayer

Take a moment to conclude your time of reflection with prayer in the space provided.

<u>Chapter 3</u>: Secrets from the Scarecrow (Page 24)

In the beginning of this chapter, we talk about how scarecrows are supposed to protect the seed from the adversary. The Bible says in Mark 4 that the seed often represents God's Word. Why do you think the adversary tries so hard to steal the Word of God from our hearts? Can you think of specific ways he has tried to steal it from your heart?

_____

_____

_____

_____

_____

_____

_____

_____

In Luke 10, Jesus also refers to the seed and harvest as lost souls that need to be brought to Him. How often do you pause to thank God for sending Jesus to protect you from the enemy until He could reap you into the harvest?

_____

_____

_____

_____

_____

Who are you being a scarecrow for? Is there anyone whom you are praying for, asking that God would save them and draw them in from the field? If not, can you identify anyone who might need you to intercede on their behalf in this way?

_____

_____

_____

_____

_____

_____

_____

While living our everyday lives, it is easy to forget we have an eternal home in Heaven. How will you use this reality to motivate you to share your faith and testimony more often?

_____

_____

_____

_____

_____

_____

_____

If I Only Had a Brain (Page 31)
We learn in this portion of the book that the most precious commodity an individual can have is his or her mind. If you lose your mind, you've lost it all. In what ways has your mind been attacked? How did it affect your life and the lives of those close to you?

_____

_____

_____

_____

_____

_____

_____

Satan wants your mind to be fixed on yourself, your circumstances and your past sin, but God wants your mind fixed on your purpose, His promises and the future plans He has in store for you. How has this chapter challenged you to protect your mind and stay focused on living with the mind of Christ?

_____

_____

_____

_____

_____

_____

_____

One Willing Heart and Two Weak Knees (Page 33)

No matter how strong we may be and no matter how much willpower we may have, all of us know what it means to be hung up in some sort of sin or weight. How does it feel to know that because Jesus was hung on a tree, just like the scarecrow, we have freedom from all of our past, present and future failures? Do you believe that? If not, what is inhibiting you from walking in that truth?

_____

_____

_____

_____

_____

_____

_____

_____

Do you sometimes feel as though you can't walk into your future because of the hang ups of your past?

_____

_____

_____

_____

_____

_____

Are you generally patient with yourself when your knees get weak to sin, or do you readily condemned yourself when you fall? If condemnation is how you typically respond, what would it take for you to instead receive God's grace and forgiveness quickly, rather than walking in your failures?

_____

_____

_____

_____

_____

_____

_____

_____

How has this chapter taught you to keep moving forward though you may have weak knees in the process?

_____

_____

_____

_____

_____

_____

_____

_____

What was the most significant lesson you learned from this portion of the chapter? How will you apply it to your life?

_____

_____

_____

_____

_____

_____

_____

_____

My Destiny Prayer
Take a moment to conclude your time of reflection with prayer in the space provided.

_____

_____

_____

_____

_____

_____

_____

_____

_____

_____

_____

_____

_____

_____

_____

_____

_____

_____

<u>Chapter 4</u>: Testimonies of the Tin Man (Page 37)

In this chapter, we learn of a Tin Man who is rusted and stuck in between where he's been and where he wants to be, all because of a storm. Describe a time in life when you felt like you were stuck and seemingly couldn't move forward.

_____

_____

_____

_____

_____

_____

_____

What happened in you or to you that placed you in that situation?

_____

_____

_____

_____

_____

_____

_____

How do you generally deal with the feeling of being stagnant and stuck?

_____

_____

_____

_____

_____

_____

_____

_____

The Need for Oil (Page 38)

The oil can that the Tin Man needed to help him move out of his situation was less than five feet away from him, yet he was too rusted to reach it. Describe a time when you knew your help was near, but you just didn't have the strength to reach it.

_____

_____

_____

_____

_____

_____

_____

_____

How frustrating is it to be able to see what you need to move forward yet you don't have the ability to reach it?

_____

_____

_____

_____

_____

_____

_____

Dorothy makes the difficult choice to delay her own destiny to help the Tin Man reach his. Have you had the experience of being stuck in life and had someone make a sacrifice to assist you? How did their action impact you?

_____

_____

_____

_____

_____

_____

_____

_____

Share a time when you did the same for others, and explain how it made you feel.

_____

_____

_____

_____

_____

_____

_____

_____

In scripture oil always refers to the anointing or the supernatural power of God. Do you often depend upon God's anointing on your life when you are experiencing trials, or do you generally try to work it out yourself? Explain.

_____

_____

_____

_____

_____

_____

_____

_____

Describe a time when you were completely dependent on the anointing of God. What were the results that followed? If you cannot recall a time, consider and explain why you think you have never depended on God, and His power, in this way.

_____

_____

_____

_____

_____

_____

_____

_____

If Only Had a Heart (Page 44)
The Tin Man accompanies Dorothy and the Scarecrow to the Emerald City in pursuit of a heart. We are often consumed with working on the external things of life, yet never stop to inspect the condition of our hearts. When you think of the word "heart" as it pertains to your destiny, what other words come to mind?

_____

_____

_____

_____

_____

_____

How important do you think it is for us to have a pure heart as we seek out our destinies?

_____

_____

_____

_____

_____

_____

_____

Describe a time in your life when you were doing the rights things, but you weren't doing them with a pure heart.

_____

_____

_____

_____

_____

_____

_____

What did you learn from the Tin Man concerning the importance of seeking a pure heart?

_____

_____

_____

_____

_____

_____

_____

What was the most powerful truth that you learned from this chapter? How will you apply it to your life?

_____

_____

_____

_____

_____

_____

_____

_____

My Destiny Prayer

Take a moment to conclude your time of reflection with prayer in the space provided.

_____

_____

_____

_____

_____

_____

_____

_____

_____

_____

_____

_____

_____

_____

_____

_____

_____

_____

Daryl W. Arnold

120

<u>Chapter 5</u>: **Lessons from the Cowardly Lion** (Page 49)

This chapter shares the story of a timid lion who is in desperate need of courage. He is consumed with anxiety and fear. How do you think being consumed with fear can affect your ability to walk in destiny?

_____

_____

_____

_____

_____

_____

_____

_____

Did you realize that allowing yourself to be consumed with fear is an actual sin against God? How will you respond to that knowledge?

_____

_____

_____

_____

_____

_____

_____

The Lion first tries his best to hide his fear by trying to terrorize Dorothy and her friends. In what ways do you try to mask the fear that is within you?

_____

_____

_____

_____

_____

_____

_____

What are some of the things in life that produce the most fear in your heart?

_____

_____

_____

_____

_____

_____

_____

_____

Can you remember what happened in your past that initiated the fear you are dealing with presently?

_____

_____

_____

_____

_____

_____

_____

All fear comes from Satan, yet we have a choice to walk in fear or walk in faith. How will you use God's Word to build your faith and destroy your fear?

_____

_____

_____

_____

_____

_____

_____

_____

How has your personal fear impacted the lives of people around you?

_____

_____

_____

_____

_____

_____

_____

Where would you be in life if you would have confronted your fears earlier?

_____

_____

_____

_____

_____

_____

_____

_____

The Lion eventually gets over his fear and begins to walk in courage. This was all because Dorothy was there to help him with his struggle. Do you have anyone in your life with whom you feel comfortable to share your fears?

_____

_____

_____

_____

_____

_____

_____

Are you willing to move forward, even if the feeling of fear does not immediately go away, or are you content with remaining immobilized by the terror of the enemy?

_____

_____

_____

_____

_____

_____

_____

What was the most powerful truth you learned from this chapter? How will you apply it to your life?

_____

_____

_____

_____

_____

_____

_____

_____

My Destiny Prayer
Take a moment to conclude your time of reflection with prayer in the space
provided.

_____

_____

_____

_____

_____

_____

_____

_____

_____

_____

_____

_____

_____

_____

_____

_____

_____

_____

Daryl W. Arnold

<u>Chapter 6</u>: **When Witches Get Worried** (Page 59)

This chapter is centered around the enemy to your destiny. Just as God has an amazing purpose for you and desires that you reach all of your divine endeavors, the enemy equally wants to delay and destroy all God has prepared for you. Have you ever felt that there was some kind of spiritual opposition to your progress in life? Share a little bit about how that opposition has been displayed.

_____

_____

_____

_____

_____

_____

_____

_____

How do you generally handle opposition when it becomes overwhelming in your life?

_____

_____

_____

_____

_____

_____

The Shoes Win the Fight (Page 59)
We discovered that the Wicked Witch of the West wasn't really after Dorothy. What was it that she really wanted?

_____

_____

Has there been a time in your life when you knew the devil was trying his best to steal the Word of God from your heart? Describe that experience.

_____

_____

_____

_____

_____

_____

_____

_____

_____

_____

_____

_____

_____

If the enemy can convince you to give up the Word and its promises, he can destroy your destiny. Describe a time when you neglected to stand on the Word of God. What were the consequences of it?

_____

_____

_____

_____

_____

_____

_____

Share a time when you refused to give up on God's Word and His promises. What was the result of your perseverance?

_____

_____

_____

_____

_____

_____

_____

The Shoes Build Your Faith (Page 62)
Knowing that faith comes by what we hear, how important do you think it is for you to study the Bible and continue to speak what it says about your destiny?

_____

_____

_____

_____

_____

_____

_____

How will you begin to develop the spiritual discipline of meditating on God's Word and declaring it over your life and future? Be very specific and practical about how this can become part of your life.

_____

_____

_____

_____

_____

_____

_____

Why do you think God so often uses the imagery of feet in scripture to illustrate His Word?

_____

_____

_____

_____

_____

_____

_____

_____

What are some ways you can challenge yourself to not just be a hearer of the Word, or even just a quoter of the Word, but to begin to walk it out?

_____

_____

_____

_____

_____

_____

_____

_____

Bring Me the Broom (Page 65)

What does the witch's broom represent in the story?

_____

_____

_____

_____

_____

_____

_____

What are some of the things you have allowed Satan to ride on in your life throughout the years? How has it negatively impacted you?

_____

_____

_____

_____

_____

_____

_____

_____

Now that you have identified the witch's broom in your life, how and
when will you surrender it to God and move on towards your destiny?
Who will you allow to hold you accountable to burning the brooms in
your life?

_____

_____

_____

_____

_____

_____

_____

_____

The Witch, the Weapons and the Water (Page 68)
Not only does God give us His Word for spiritual warfare, He also gives
us His Spirit. The water in the story is a representation of God's Spirit.
How has depending upon the Spirit of God led you on your journey?

_____

_____

_____

_____

_____

_____

_____

Ultimately, the water was the tool that destroyed the witch. What have you been able to defeat in your life because you fought, not in the flesh, but in the Spirit?

_____

_____

_____

_____

_____

_____

_____

What resonated with you most powerfully in this chapter? How will you apply it to your life?

_____

_____

_____

_____

_____

_____

_____

_____

My Destiny Prayer

Take a moment to conclude your time of reflection with prayer in the space provided.

_____

_____

_____

_____

_____

_____

_____

_____

_____

_____

_____

_____

_____

_____

_____

_____

_____

_____

Chapter 7: The Wizard's Weakness (Page 71)

This particular chapter is about the Wizard of Oz who, supposedly, has the power to grant every wish and meet any possible need. However, we find out later in the story that he's a mere man pretending to be all-powerful. Dorothy and her friends spent their whole journey chasing a figment of their imagination.

How can you identify with Dorothy in this chapter as it pertains to putting your hope in people, places and things that have left you lost and unsatisfied? Explain.

_____

_____

_____

_____

_____

_____

_____

_____

_____

_____

_____

_____

_____

_____

Oftentimes we have put our complete trust in God-inspired systems, such as church or other religious organizations, rather than trusting in God Himself. Has there been a time when these organizations have failed you? Give an example.

_____

_____

_____

_____

_____

_____

_____

Have you ever been angry at people, because you desired for them to do for you what only God could do? Is there someone in your life right now who you have put in the place of God?

_____

_____

_____

_____

_____

_____

_____

How has this chapter taught you to think differently concerning where you put your trust?

_____

_____

_____

_____

_____

_____

_____

_____

Who will you allow to help you refocus when you begin to exalt other things above God?

_____

_____

_____

_____

_____

_____

_____

_____

How will you apply the truth of this chapter to your life?

_____

_____

_____

_____

_____

_____

_____

_____

Ask the Father to forgive you for allowing other people to sit upon the throne of your heart, a place that is supposed to be reserved for Him.

_____

_____

_____

_____

_____

_____

_____

_____

My Destiny Prayer

Take a moment to conclude your time of reflection with prayer in the space provided.

_____

_____

_____

_____

_____

_____

_____

_____

_____

_____

_____

_____

_____

_____

_____

_____

_____

Chapter 8: A Message from Man's Best Friend (Page 75)

This chapter is about the importance of having the right people in your life at the right time. How important do you think divine relationships are as you journey toward your destiny? Why?

_____

_____

_____

_____

_____

_____

_____

_____

How has having the wrong people around you affected your life?

_____

_____

_____

_____

_____

_____

_____

_____

Name a few people who have been crucial to your life's success. Why have they had such an impact? Have you shared with them just how significant your relationship with them has been?

_____

_____

_____

_____

_____

_____

_____

_____

Have you ever kept a person in your life beyond their season? What were the consequences of your unwillingness to let that person go?

_____

_____

_____

_____

_____

_____

_____

_____

The Silent Partner (Page 78)
Toto stood by Dorothy's side the entire journey without saying a word. Share a time when someone stood by your side during a painful period in life. How did you respond to their presence in that time?

_____

_____

_____

_____

_____

_____

_____

Describe a time when you had to do the same for others. How were they impacted?

_____

_____

_____

_____

_____

_____

_____

One of the measurements of a genuine friendship is that a real friend will celebrate your success without being jealous. Do you have someone with whom you can share your dreams without the fear of them being envious?

_____

_____

_____

_____

_____

_____

_____

Another measurement of genuine friendship is a person who will correct you when you are going in the wrong direction. Do you have anyone in your life like that? How does their correction affect your relationship?

_____

_____

_____

_____

_____

_____

_____

What was the most powerful truth you learned from this chapter? How will you apply it to your life?

_____

_____

_____

_____

_____

_____

_____

_____

My Destiny Prayer
Take a moment to conclude your time of reflection with prayer in the space provided.

<u>Chapter 9</u>: **Don't Miss Your Destiny** (Page 82)

This final chapter was written to encourage you to look inward to God who lives within you for joy, fulfillment and purpose, instead of looking to the external. Why do you think that is so difficult for most of us?

_____

_____

_____

_____

_____

_____

_____

Do you think you have been looking outside of yourself for success and fulfillment, when in all actuality, God has put everything you need on the inside of you? Explain why.

_____

_____

_____

_____

_____

_____

_____

What insecurities have kept you from believing you are God's best?

_____

_____

_____

_____

_____

_____

_____

_____

What will you do to start resolving those false insecurities and start building yourself up?

_____

_____

_____

_____

_____

_____

_____

_____

Has reading this book revealed some things in you internally that need to change if you are to reach your destiny? What are they?

_____

_____

_____

_____

_____

_____

_____

Enjoying the Journey (Page 86)
Have you defined destiny as something that will come in the near future, rather than seeing destiny as a daily walk with God?

_____

_____

_____

_____

_____

_____

_____

_____

How would your life be different if you began to see destiny as a daily walk with God as opposed to a distant place in the future?

_____

_____

_____

_____

_____

_____

_____

_____

Describe three practical things that you will do to begin to enjoy the journey God has for you.

_____

_____

_____

_____

_____

_____

_____

_____

What was the most powerful truth that you learned from this chapter? How will you apply it to your life?

_____

_____

_____

_____

_____

_____

_____

_____

My Destiny Prayer
Take a moment to conclude your time of reflection with prayer in the space provided.

_____

_____

_____

_____

_____

_____

_____

_____

_____

_____

_____

_____

_____

_____

_____

_____

Acknowledgments

"I've learned that you shouldn't go through life with a catcher's mitt on both hands. You need to be able to throw something back."
– Maya Angelou

I am writing this dedication from the top of one of the most beautiful mountain peaks north of Beirut, Lebanon. Who would have thought the youngest child of five raised by a single mom would be authoring a book? I actually struggled with reading most of my childhood. How can a person go from fighting through grade school and barely graduating from high school to having speaking opportunities in countries all over the world? It is no less than the grace of God and the selfless people He has put in my life. Therefore, I would be in eternal error not to take this time to acknowledge at least a few people who have played a significant role in my success.

First, to God who has blessed me far beyond my obedience and righteousness. Your Word has been evident in my life time and again. When I have been faithless, you have been faithful, because you cannot deny yourself. Thank you for inspiring this book by the Holy Spirit. Use it for Your glory that many might come to know your son, Jesus the Christ, as their Lord and Savior.

To my mother, Cladie Arnold, who raised me and my siblings to believe that obstacles in life could become stepping stones if we would just put them under our feet. Thank you, momma, for loving me and believing in me when I didn't have enough sense to believe in myself. Thank you for teaching me the things of God and keeping me around a Christian culture. Thank you for being the best example I have ever seen of perseverance and determination. You are one of the greatest gifts in God's creation.

To my beautiful wife, Carmeisha. You are the reason I wake up in the mornings. You have been the epitome of God's grace in my life. Your love for me is much more than I had ever prayed for. God put you in my life because He knew I would never become the best me without having you in it. You undoubtedly have made me better. You, ma'am, are the love of God personified. When I found you, I found a good thing. Thank you for being a model of integrity to my children and raising them to become the jewels they were destined to be. I love you more than words can express.

To my children, Daisha, Chania, Timbreland, and Azariah. You are the exception to the rule. You have broken every preacher's kid stereotype. You have sacrificed and served God with honor. I couldn't ask for better children. Thank you for standing strong under the pressure of life and not compromising during the journey. Thank you for being patient with me when I didn't always offer the same to you. Thank you for sharing me with the world even though you never signed up for this. God will always reward you for your faithfulness. Know your daddy loves you dearly, and I am very proud of you all.

To Overcoming Believers Church. You are the apple of my eye. God has used you as a tool in His hand to build His kingdom here on Earth. Your commitment to the vision and your steadfast service to Jesus has been an example to churches and Christians all over the world. Thank you for believing in the God in me even when the vision was sometimes unclear. May the blessing of the Lord make you rich in every area of your lives. God gets the glory, many times I get the credit, but I pray that you will get the reward in heaven for all you have done. Remember, you are an overcomer by the blood of the Lamb and by the word of your testimony. Love not your life unto death.

To many others who have encouraged me along the way to expose my gifts to the world – my pastoral friends and covenant bothers, my spiritual sons and daughters, my mentors and role models. To my editor, Ms. Kellye Coleman. Thank you for the many hours of discussion we have had while trying to put this book together. May the Father open the windows of Heaven and pour out blessings you do not have room to receive.

About the Author

Pastor Daryl W. Arnold is the Founder and Senior Pastor of Overcoming Believers Church in Knoxville, Tenn. He and his wife, Lady Carmeisha Arnold, are divinely called to inspire Believers to live the abundant life and to empower them to walk in the fullness of their Kingdom assignments. Although Pastor Arnold is known internationally for his revelatory preaching and his passion for the Word of God, he is most passionate about serving the Knoxville community.

Pastor Arnold is a graduate of Knoxville College where he earned his B.S. degree in Business Management and Marketing. He is a member of Kappa Alpha Psi Fraternity, Inc. He was the first Board Chair for Girl Talk Inc. and presently serves on the Knoxville City Mayor's Save Our Sons (S.O.S) Task Force under the umbrella of My Brother's Keeper, initiated by former, President Barack Obama. He serves as a Task Force Member for the Knox County School Superintendent for Disparities in Educational Outcomes. He served on the Steering Committee for Community Connectors Knoxville under the umbrella of CEO for Cities. Pastor Arnold serves as the Co-Chair of the Change Center Knoxville and is a board member of the Trinity Health Foundation.

A native of Chattanooga, Tenn., Pastor Arnold's greatest joy is his beautiful wife of over two decades, Carmeisha, and his four children. His hands are on his ministry, but his heart is on his family.

Made in the USA
Lexington, KY
27 June 2017